Dear Reader:

AMI Books is p[...]
exciting new series straight from th[...]
The National Enquirer, America's favorite
tabloid. Now, every month, we will be going
in-depth to bring you the whole story.

The book you are about to read is based on
the work of some of the top award-winning
investigative journalists in the world. If
you're looking for the inside scoop on topics
ranging from the most sensational crimes
captivating our nation to Hollywood profiles
that show the tragedy under the tinsel, you'll
find it here.

For over thirty years, *The National
Enquirer* has been telling it like it is to more
than thirteen million readers a week — and
now we're going to take you deep into the
Enquirer's confidential files to bring you the
untold stories behind the headlines.

Valerie Virga
President, AMI Books

From the files of
The National Enquirer

They're Killing Our Children

By MICHELLE CARUSO and NICHOLAS MAIER

American Media Inc.

FROM THE FILES OF THE NATIONAL ENQUIRER:
THEY'RE KILLING OUR CHILDREN

Copyright © 2002 AMI Books, Inc.

Cover design: Martin Elfers
Cover photograph of Danielle van Dam: Courtesy van Dam family/ZUMA Press; Miranda Gaddis: AP Wide World Photos/Eric Cable; Ashley Pond: Getty Images; Samantha Runnion: Courtesy of Runnion family/ZUMA Press; Elizabeth Smart: Joy Gough/ZUMA Press

ISBN: 1-885840-02-0

First printing: December, 2002

Printed in the United States of America

10 9 8 7 6 5 4 3 2 1

FORWARD

Their young faces are forever burned into our memories — snapshots from family photo albums of children, bright-eyed and happy. They are at birthday parties, at school, and on the playground. We see home videos of them riding horses, selling Girl Scout cookies, and going to church. But the tragic reason we share in these intimate memories is only because the unthinkable has occurred — these kids have been taken from their homes and brutally raped and murdered. From the best of times, when least expected, comes pain and death. Our worst nightmare becomes reality.

Almost daily we hear of another case of kidnapping, followed by stories of sexual abuse and violence. Decomposed bodies and tiny skeletons are found in desolate places, mysteries resolved with details of last moments spent in terror. In communities both upper and lower class, in neighborhoods of all ethnic backgrounds, these are the worst kinds of crimes. Our kids are being stolen, and with each subsequent case, a part of our collective soul is lost forever.

According to the National Center for Missing and Exploited Children (NCMEC) in Alexandria, Virginia, each year more than 750,000 children are reported missing in the United States. Most are simply lost, have run away from home, or have been taken by parents involved in bitter custody fights. Still, more than 50,000 fall into a category called "non-family" abductions. Out of those, there are roughly a hundred cases that result in the worst outcome — murder.

Ernie Allen, the president of the NCMEC, explains that half of the children on this final list at any time are under the age of thirteen and that two-thirds are girls. Allen describes the typical victim as an eleven-year-old from a stable, middle-class family. The abductions tend to take place in warmer states, such as California and Texas, where children spend more time outdoors, although no state has proved immune. Often victims come into contact with their abductor within a quarter mile of their home.

Allen points out that the concept of a "dirty old man," of some easily identifiable assailant, is a myth. The vast majority of these crimes are committed by males who are thirty-five or younger. The predators are insidious, intelligent, and often patient, willing to do whatever it takes to work their way into positions of trust where they can carry out their diabolical plans. They ingratiate themselves into the lives of unsuspecting families. States Allen, "They become familiar in order to be able to quietly lure children."

The individual cases are almost too numerous to list, but a few stand out. Danielle van Dam was seven years old, blonde and green-eyed, with a wide, inviting smile. Ashley Pond and Miranda Gaddis were two friends, twelve and thirteen, both striking and vibrant. Then came Samantha Runnion, the very picture of perfection, a beautiful five-year-old girl. In every photograph she is smiling, her brown eyes filled with light. Everyone who saw her felt that light, which only compounded the darkness to follow. Each of these girls was kidnapped and killed — four victims of many when even one becomes too much to take.

If any encouragement can be derived from these examples, at least arrests have been made and some closure afforded the tortured parents. David Westerfield has been convicted of taking Danielle van Dam from her home in the middle of the night and murdering her. The bodies of Ashley Pond and Miranda Gaddis were found on the property of Ward Weaver III, their neighbor. Alejandro Avila is awaiting trial for the rape and murder of Samantha Runnion. All suspects are innocent until proven guilty, but with each of these crimes, clues to the trends can already be revealed and lessons, however hard, learned.

What inevitably stays with all of us are those snapshots of the victims shown on the evening news and in the morning papers. They cause us to care and to cry, and they pull at our hearts like nothing else. But these snapshots are also what proved to be the victims' undoing. To a child killer, a monster of the worst kind lurking among us, that very innocence attracts pure evil.

A Wolf in Sheep's Clothing

CHAPTER 1

Little Danielle van Dam was born in Texas before her parents settled into a four-bedroom, beige stucco contemporary home in a quiet neighborhood in upscale Sabre Springs, California. The small town is a suburban oasis twenty miles north of San Diego, with only four thousand residents, tree-lined streets, and carefully landscaped gardens. Danielle's father, Damon, worked as a software engineer for the telecommunications company Qualcomm, while her mother, Brenda, stayed at home to raise Danielle and her two brothers, Derrick, age ten, and Dylen, five. They were, by all appearances, the perfect family living the American dream.

On a video of the energetic young girl at Disneyland clowning with her family, Danielle's constant broad, gap-toothed grin bespoke her affable and social personality. Pink and purple, the little girl's favorite colors, lined her small bedroom on the second floor of the van Dam home. A plastic toy box rested at the foot of a canopied poster bed with lilac sheets, and against a wall sat a shiny white dresser, stuffed with her beaded and colorful clothes, some of which also spilled out of a large closet. The floor was covered with purple carpeting, and a desk displayed family photos. Everywhere were her treasured dolls, and from the ceiling hung little fluffy hearts.

Danielle's teachers at Creekside Elementary School, where she was in the second grade, described her as a typical seven-year-old — learning to read, eating in the cafeteria with her many friends, and writing a speech on "sharing" about a family vacation.

Amy DeStefanie, who taught Danielle in kindergarten and first grade, recalled, "She got along with everybody. Everybody was Danielle's friend. She never wanted anyone to feel alone or sad.

"Danielle was a very sweet, polite, hard-working little girl. She really enjoyed school. She really enjoyed doing her best and learning new things. She really liked — I remember very strongly that she liked to write . . . She would write about what her family did over the weekend. She would write about her friends. She would write imaginative stories, practice new words, hard words, try to spell words that she didn't know for sure how to spell."

Damon recalled other details about Danielle. She enjoyed working with her father in the garage, helping as he tinkered with the car. They would also do woodworking, and she'd make "abstract art," as Damon affectionately called it. They even made a birdhouse, which still sits in their garage, unpainted.

"She loved spending time one-on-one with me like that."

Damon filmed a dance recital of little Danielle performing with all her classmates. "They'd have the Britney Spears music . . . She was just so thrilled to go, so happy to be onstage and get dressed up in her dance outfit."

She also spent a lot of time with her two brothers. "She was teaching her younger brother to read before bed," said

Damon. "I would just sit and listen to her read to him and help her out.

"My favorite thing with her was she'd give me the big squeezy hug. I don't know how it started, but she just — she was really strong and she'd give a real tight squeeze hug and I'd pretend to fall dead and go limp, and she'd just giggle and laugh and thought it was the funniest thing that she could squeeze so hard."

Brenda described Danielle as being "very loving and kind. She always cared about how other people felt. And I've always — I've always told them [her children] to treat others how you would want to be treated, and so she was just very loving and kind to other people."

One of the most important hobbies for Danielle was being a Daisy. As Brenda explained, "Daisies is the first form of Brownies, and then eventually you go to Girl Scouts, so she wanted to join Daisies. We joined Daisies, and then in first grade she bridged to Brownies."

Brenda was the "cookie mom" for the troop, which meant it fell to her to keep the cartons of Girl Scout cookies in her garage, give them out to the girls, and then take in all the money. She recalled going door-to-door with Danielle selling them. The smiling tyke always managed to unload boxes and boxes upon adoring neighbors.

On one such fateful trip, Danielle and her brother, Dylen, rang the bell of their neighbor, David Westerfield, a self-employed engineer who lived only two doors down. Although the van Dams recognized him and had often exchanged polite hellos, Westerfield took the opportunity to introduce himself formally to Danielle's mother, an attractive blonde.

While the children ran around his pool, Westerfield quickly bought four boxes of cookies. With piercing dark eyes, the hulking six-foot-two, 210-pound man also cast a long and hard second glance toward Danielle van Dam. Brenda had no clue at the time what true evil lurked behind this man's pleasant and affable facade. He was, as so many would later describe, a normal, friendly neighbor — the same type that all of us know and trust.

On the evening of Friday, February 1, 2002, the van Dam family sat down in the dining room at their naturally stained wood table and ate pizza together, recounting their day while swapping stories and laughs. It was a festive night, and they all looked forward to the weekend.

Danielle had been especially excited about the van Dams' upcoming trip to Italy. She had her passport photo taken that afternoon. Besides that, there was the father/daughter school dance scheduled for the following Thursday. For the event, themed "Be a Star," her mom had bought her a new sparkly pants outfit, its blouse embellished with a star.

By eight o'clock, two friends of the parents, Barbara Easton and Denise Kemal, arrived at the house. They had scheduled a "girls' night out," and they started the party by going out into the garage to smoke marijuana, where the van Dams had reversed the lock so their children wouldn't catch them unexpectedly. Little did Brenda know then that the sordid details of her freewheeling lifestyle would soon come under intense public scrutiny, including not only the van Dams' alcohol and drug use but also their participation in "swinging" that involved kinky sex with multiple partners.

After getting high, Brenda and her guests left to go to a local watering hole, Dad's Café, leaving Damon to baby-sit. Danielle played with the family dog, Layla, a weimaraner, before writing in her journal at the dining room table. Damon drank a third beer and played video games with his sons. The father recalled tucking his children into their respective beds by 10:30 p.m., and when he went into

Danielle's room, she was already comfy under the covers, wearing blue flowered pajamas.

"I gave her a kiss goodnight," said Damon, adding that he left all of the kids' doors open a few inches, a cautionary habit that allowed him to hear if any of them needed him during the night. After watching more television and walking the dog, he also went to bed.

Across town at Dad's, Brenda, Denise and Barbara were drinking and "dirty dancing" with one another. The women enjoyed the attention their provocative moves garnered from the men — it was all part of a typical girls' night out for the friends. One man who seemed fixated by the display was the van Dams' neighbor, David Westerfield, who had been there when the women arrived. He offered to buy them drinks and they accepted.

"He said, 'Ladies don't buy their own drinks,' and threw some money on the counter," remembered Brenda, who admitted to having three cranberry and vodka cocktails and a shot of tequila. The women also left the bar briefly to smoke more marijuana in Brenda's SUV.

Despite the impending swirl of unwanted publicity and controversy surrounding the parents, Westerfield would eventually emerge as the true villain. Denise Kemal, one of the friends at Dad's with Brenda, noticed him that evening standing nearby and staring at them ominously. "I thought to myself, 'Wow, that's creepy that he's just standing there watching,' " said Kemal, a twenty-eight-year-old flight attendant with Southwest Airlines.

At 1:50 Saturday morning, the women, now accompanied by two male friends, left Dad's as it closed. Despite her drinking, Brenda drove. Although witnesses would debate the precise time of Westerfield's departure, all agree that he had already left the bar by that point.

Back at their home, Damon van Dam awoke to let the dog

out and noticed a burglar alarm light blinking when his wife
and the others arrived. Brenda recalled that a door in the
garage was ajar and went to investigate. Because the parents
had reversed the lock from the garage into the house to
prevent their children from catching them when they smoked
marijuana, someone coming in from the garage could have
easily gained entrance. Meanwhile, as Brenda closed the
garage door, Denise went upstairs with Damon, where they
"kissed and rubbed each other," as Damon later admitted.

After eating pizza, the guests left and the van Dams went
to bed at 2:30 a.m. without checking on their children. The
parents had already closed each child's door so as not to
disturb them with the adults' late night "conversation." They
had no reason to suspect the unthinkable.

At 3 a.m., Damon awoke once more to use the
bathroom and noticed that their alarm now indicated there
was another open door or window somewhere in the house.
When he went to investigate, he found a sliding glass door
open. The parents would eventually theorize that Westerfield
had come in through the garage, hidden inside their home,
and then snuck out the back with Danielle. That evening,
however, Damon assumed only that one of his wife's friends
had left the sliding glass door open, which he closed before
returning to bed.

"I didn't check on the kids. I was tired and I didn't think
that door being open was important at the time," he said.
Later Damon admitted that had been a "mistake," one he
would forever regret making.

The next morning, after the rest of the family was up and
starting their day, a neighbor dropped off her two kids at the
van Dam house. Brenda had agreed beforehand to baby-sit,
and she went up to Danielle's room to wake her daughter to
join her friends and have breakfast. Upon opening her door,
she noticed Danielle's canopied poster bed was empty and

the bed unmade. There was no sign of her little girl.

"We started looking everywhere," said the mother, describing her state of mind at the time as frantic. "I started looking around the house and looking in the closets, but we couldn't find her."

As their search proved fruitless, Brenda dialed 911. An emergency operator named Diane answered the call.

"Yes, ma'am," Brenda said, trying to remain calm for a second before just blurting out, "My daughter's not in her bed this morning. She's only seven!"

"Just now?" asked Diane.

"Just now. I thought she was in there sleeping . . . she's not there."

"She doesn't have any history of running away or anything, right?"

"No, no, not at all and, and . . . oh my gosh."

"All right, take a deep breath, okay?"

"Did you find her?" Distracted and growing panicked, Brenda yelled out to her husband, "Is she anywhere?"

"What's your daughter's name?" the dispatcher asked, trying to keep Brenda's attention.

"Danielle."

"And her last name is the same?"

"Van Dam . . . She has brown short hair, we just had it cut, it's right to her shoulders . . . Um, she's probably about sixty pounds. And um . . . um, I don't know how tall. I don't, I just can't . . ." Screaming to her husband again, Brenda asked, "How tall is she? How tall is she, Damon? I don't know where she could be."

"Okay, how tall are you, ma'am?" The operator asked.

"I'm five-four," answered Brenda.

"Okay, and . . . and . . . and is she how much shorter than you, do you think?"

"She comes up to my chest."

"So she's probably about four . . . four foot, probably about, what, eight?"

"Yeah. Yeah. Maybe a little shorter."

"Probably about sixty pounds, right?"

"Yeah."

"What color eyes?"

"Um, they're green."

As Brenda spoke, the voices of the other children looking for Danielle could be heard in the background.

"It doesn't look like anybody broke through the house or anything?" asked Diane.

"There was a door open in the house, but . . . but . . . um, I didn't check the bed and um . . . I came home about two. And my husband was home with them. He was home. And he said good night to them, and I guess he went to sleep. The back door was cracked, he said. The back door and the side garage door, he found the back door cracked. Oh my gosh."

"Okay, ma'am, we have an officer coming there . . . Take a deep breath and calm down. It sounds like you have other kids there."

"I have my husband and two other children, and . . . and my neighbor just brought her kids over. I need to call her so she can come back and get them."

"Okay. Think positive thoughts and everything will be okay..."

CHAPTER 2

Within minutes of Brenda van Dam's call to 911, scores of officers from the San Diego Police Department were pulling into the usually serene Sabre Springs neighborhood. Some spoke with the distraught parents while others searched the surrounding area. Crime scene analysts began collecting any potential evidence from the home. Danielle would never run away, Brenda tearfully maintained, even though she knew the alternative was far worse.

In a matter of hours, the police were followed by a parade of media satellite trucks. Cameramen and reporters clogged the streets and lawns, broadcasting live stories of the van Dams' painful loss around the world. As if America needed another reminder that we were no longer safe at home, Danielle's kidnapping would be only the first of 2002 to captivate our nation.

From the outset, the lead investigator on the case was Lieutenant Jim Collins, a seasoned veteran of the SDPD, who worked under Police Chief David Bejarano. Detectives immediately recognized a suspicious fact after canvassing all of the van Dams' neighbors: Only one was gone at the time the police arrived at the scene — David Westerfield.

Arousing suspicions further, a woman who lived in the lot behind Westerfield volunteered to police that when she awoke at 2:30 in the morning, his home was "closed up and every single blind was shut tight." The neighbor, Christina Hoeffs, added that she had never noticed this before.

Sergeant Johnny Keene and his partner, Maura Parga, two officers assigned to the department's robbery and kidnapping unit, were told to speak with David Westerfield as soon as he returned. Staring at his two-story beige stucco home, which looked like every other house on the block, Parga noticed a garden hose haphazardly strewn across the otherwise immaculately manicured lawn.

"It told me whoever left that hose was in a hurry," said Parga. "Because the yard was so neat, it just didn't seem right."

The detectives also learned from neighbors that Westerfield had, in fact, returned briefly during the day Saturday, standing with the crowds and observing the masses of police and media. Three separate witnesses saw his RV in the neighborhood later that day, around four o'clock in the afternoon, cruising slowly down the street as if the driver wanted to soak in the sights, admiring the commotion.

The following Monday morning, the detectives got their chance to follow up on their hunch. As Brenda and Damon van Dam offered a $25,000 reward for information leading to Danielle's return and searchers combed a twenty-five-mile radius around their home, stretching from Mexico to the desert east of San Diego, Keene and Parga approached Westerfield on the sidewalk in front of his house. By this point, they knew Westerfield had been arrested for drunk driving in 1996, but he had no known violent criminal history.

As they began to talk, Westerfield acknowledged knowing the van Dams, but not intimately. He mentioned how he had bought Girl Scout cookies from Danielle and had also seen Brenda at Dad's Café, where the two discussed her little girl. Westerfield told the detectives he learned Danielle had a new dress to attend a father/daughter dance and that Damon, according to Brenda, thought his daughter was "growing up too fast." Shortly after returning home Friday night, Westerfield claimed, he went to bed.

Said Keene of that first encounter, "I noticed he [Westerfield] was sweating profusely." Both Keene and his partner explained that the winter morning was cold, estimating the temperature to be about fifty degrees. Parga claimed to be shivering under a thick jacket even as Westerfield, wearing only a cotton shirt and jeans, was saturated with perspiration.

When Keene asked Westerfield about where he had been, their suspect launched into a convoluted story about a trip in his RV. He supposedly started out first thing Saturday morning and drove from the beach to the mountains to the desert and then back to the beach. The journey included more than a dozen different stops and one trip back to his home because he claimed to have lost his wallet.

Keene immediately recognized that a few aspects of Westerfield's story didn't make sense. Westerfield described in detail driving a twisty route from Glamis in the desert to Coronado on the ocean in little more than an hour. The trip is ninety miles long, and due to the winding roads, it takes three hours. The various hunches the investigators had were beginning to add up.

When Keene noticed that Westerfield's hands were covered with small cuts, the suspect quickly explained that his RV had gotten stuck in the desert and he had tried to dig it out. Eventually, a tow-truck driver was called to help, and Westerfield was back on the road again.

Westerfield also appeared "overly cooperative," according to the detectives. He signed papers allowing them to search his home and RV without a warrant, even guiding officers through the home and pointing out closets they had missed. Parga and Keene noticed a strong odor of bleach and a bed comforter on top of the dryer in the garage, raising suspicions that a thorough cleaning had been attempted before they showed up.

"Nothing was out of place," noted Keene.

Added Parga, "Everything was very neat, very clean."

During that cursory search of his home and the RV, Westerfield admitted to the detectives he had cleaned and vacuumed his motor home and had taken some items to the dry cleaner. The detectives left, fully aware they would be back again soon.

No sooner was he alone again than Westerfield enthusiastically agreed to do an interview with a local television station on his front lawn.

"Why were they interviewing you?" asked the reporter, who had noticed the investigators leaving Westerfield's home.

"You'd have to ask them. I was gone all weekend and I offered to let them look through everything. This isn't going to be on TV, is it?" Westerfield then asked. Smiling, the balding man joked, "At least let me put my hat on!"

As Westerfield enjoyed his newfound fame, another detective showed up at the Twin Peaks Dry Cleaners and learned that the suspect had dropped off clothes, including a jacket, and bedding.

"He wouldn't look me in the eye," said Julie Mills, one of the Twin Peaks employees who had helped Westerfield.

Added Kelly Belom, another worker who was there when

Westerfield came in, "He was acting very different than he usually does. He's usually very talkative and outgoing and smiles a lot."

Later that day, a police interrogation specialist named Paul Redden interviewed Westerfield again. Most of the taped conversation revolved around what had already been discussed with Keene and Parga earlier that morning. Investigators often try to go over minute details repeatedly with suspects in an effort to uncover inconsistencies in fabricated stories. It's easiest to tell the truth, while lying often requires a photographic memory, especially with an alibi as complex as the one Westerfield had presented.

Recounting that strange trip to more than a dozen places during the weekend, Westerfield admitted, "This whole story sounds weird to everybody else, but it makes perfect sense to me."

After Redden asked Westerfield what he thought might have happened to Danielle, he replied that possibly she had just walked away from her home to play with friends. Once again he mentioned buying the Girl Scout cookies from the little girl, but added, "If you brought her in right now, I wouldn't be able to tell her from ten [other] kids."

Regarding the night of Danielle's disappearance and Westerfield's conversations with Brenda at Dad's Café, Redden asked, "Were you hitting on [Brenda] at all?"

"She's not my type," Westerfield replied, commenting that Brenda was "kind of heavyset."

Most notably, at least once during that conversation, Westerfield's story changed from the singular to the plural, or from "I" to "we," when talking about his trip. In describing a desert area known as Borrego, he said, "This little place we were at . . ."

CHAPTER 3

The following Tuesday morning, Brenda van Dam appeared on the *Today* show. The grieving and emotionally drained mother pleaded for Danielle's return. The four days since her daughter was abducted had been the longest and hardest of her life. Her face was drawn and tired.

"Just drop her off and leave and let her come home to us," she begged. "Our only concern is getting her back. We just want our baby back."

For the van Dams, this was another opportunity to try to keep public interest in their daughter alive as precious hours ticked by. If there was a chance that someone watching might have information about Danielle's whereabouts, then the media attention could be used to the parents' advantage. If something, *anything*, could help, the van Dams were prepared to do it.

By this point, as many families faced with such a crisis do, Brenda and Damon had enlisted the help of a spokesperson and an attorney to coordinate their game plan. To offset inevitable questions of the parents' potential involvement,

Brenda had even agreed to submit to a police-administered lie-detector test, which she passed.

Meanwhile, the SDPD detectives were progressing with their investigation, although they gave no hints that Westerfield had become a main suspect. As police questioned registered sex offenders in the area, searched more than two hundred homes, followed up on nearly a thousand tips, and combed every square inch of the surrounding area, police spokesperson Dave Cohen said only, "We have no reason to believe she walked away. We would have found her already if that was the case."

The FBI, who had freely offered their assistance, were not directly involved as there was no evidence that Danielle van Dam had been taken out of state, which would have made the kidnapping a federal crime. Their forensic labs were available, as well as their teams of expert profilers. For the time being, they would stay in the background and let the SDPD do their job.

The same day Brenda van Dam appeared on the *Today* show, Westerfield was hit with a warrant to search his home. This would not be a casual walk-through like the first search Westerfield consented to. The warrant described in detail items to be taken — any child pornography or jewelry Danielle had been wearing when she went to bed February 1, including a plastic choker, or tight necklace, and Mickey Mouse earrings. Police also sought any "binding materials," such as tape, rope, or "leather collars."

Police seized both Westerfield's RV and SUV, impounding them for further analysis, and carted off more than a dozen boxes and garbage bags full of other belongings. The jacket and bedding he had dry-cleaned were taken. A team of forensic crime scene analysts descended on the home, collecting dryer lint, trash and searching for minute fiber and DNA evidence. Westerfield was also forced to lead investigators on another trip tracing the one he had claimed to make the weekend of Danielle's disappearance.

Suddenly, with the media hounding the police department, Lt. Jim Collins admitted, "We have been focusing on him, but I'm not going to characterize him as a prime suspect."

Investigators often keep their hand closely guarded, and only when it's advantageous, or, in this case, blatantly obvious, do they lay their cards down. After all, they already knew Westerfield had attempted an extensive "cleaning" of his property. Detectives didn't want him destroying any more evidence before they were prepared, as they were now, to take anything and everything that could possibly link their suspect to the crime.

By Thursday, Westerfield had wisely hired Steven Feldman, a defense attorney with more than two decades of experience. Feldman had once worked on a death penalty case where he won an acquittal for a man accused of murder who had spent more than five years in jail awaiting trial. In addition to defending Westerfield, Feldman would also serve as a mouthpiece for his client. There would be no more interviews with the suspect like the one on his front lawn. The lawyer initially declined even to discuss the case with reporters, saying only, "There's an ongoing investigation."

The day after he hired Feldman, Westerfield was suddenly receiving help from another source, the media, who were feeding a public infatuation with emerging details of the van Dams' "swinging" lifestyle. Although Brenda and Damon van Dam eventually came clean to investigators about their "alternative" habits, their public evasiveness only fueled that fire. The fact that the police had stated the parents were not suspects didn't offset any of the attention.

That Friday, a local radio talk-show host, Rick Roberts, dedicated a four-hour show to reports that Danielle's parents sometimes had "sex parties" at their Sabre Springs home.

According to unidentified sources that came forward, Brenda and Damon arranged trysts with other couples through an Internet club called C.B.'s and also during chance meetings in local bars.

While Brenda had said publicly that she went home from Dad's Café at 2 a.m. with a few friends to have a "pizza supper," other people in the bar questioned her account.

"Pizza my foot!" one regular said. "They probably went back to her house to have sex. That's what Brenda and Damon do for fun. They meet people and bring them home to have sex. Brenda's the bait. She goes out with her friends who are in the swingers' group, while Damon stays home to put the kids to bed. Then she brings the crowd home."

The source claimed Brenda once asked him, "Are you a swinger?" But when he replied that he and his wife were not, the mother just shrugged and never approached him again.

Another regular at Dad's detailed accepting an invitation to the van Dam home. "Brenda is very alluring," disclosed the source. "She even turns playing pool in the bar into a sexy game. When I went to her home with a group of people, she chose me as her partner. Damon hooked up with one of the women. I was nervous, but I could see that Brenda and Damon were used to having group sex. They went about it so matter-of-factly.

"It's all kind of a blur. I mostly remember a lot of naked bodies everywhere. Although some people changed partners, I stuck with Brenda and she wore me out."

While the van Dams appealed for help to find Danielle, talk-show host Rick Roberts had sparked a fresh media frenzy. Reporters relentlessly pursued any and all of the sordid details. There was growing speculation that the van Dams' lifestyle had contributed to the little girl's abduction.

One acquaintance of the couple said, "Brenda and Damon's lifestyle creates bizarre situations — and this is what follows."

Police officials were quoted insinuating that the van Dams' failure to peek into Danielle's bedroom was a result of them being too "preoccupied" with the guests Brenda had brought home from Dad's Café. Reports of investigators following tips that Brenda may have been having a secret affair with David Westerfield emerged. Although Brenda claimed they were merely acquaintances, which proved true, witnesses came forward at the time claiming the two were "dirty dancing" at the bar on the night Danielle disappeared.

Already coping with horrendous pain, the van Dams elected to try to circumvent the new controversy. When Brenda was asked about the allegations by a reporter, she replied, "This is in no way related to the investigation."

And Steve Yunker, their attorney, argued that the allegations about the family's lifestyle threatened to obscure the most important factor. "The van Dams wish to focus on their daughter. That alone is important for them."

Thankfully for the parents, a week later, after yet another search of his premises, Westerfield was finally arrested. According to investigators, more than 64,000 pornographic images and 2,000 video clips had been found on four computers in his home. Some depicted girls having sex with animals, while others showed them in bondage. Most incriminating were photos of prepubescent girls the same age as Danielle van Dam. The pornography, according to detectives, had been tirelessly catalogued into a veritable library of filth.

There was one animated cartoon among many that especially turned the investigators' stomachs and sent chills down their spines. The digitally generated clip showed a little girl in pigtails, her hands tied behind her back, begging an adult man not to touch or hurt her. The man then lifted her arms over her head with a leather strap and stripped off her dress. As she fought to free herself, he brutally raped her.

More than a few investigators wondered if this had been a blueprint for Westerfield's actions on the night of February 1.

Although the evidence spoke volumes about Westerfield's demented interest in little girls, the resulting misdemeanor charges of possession of child pornography soon became the least of his concerns. A three-centimeter stain of little Danielle van Dam's blood had been found on a shoulder of the jacket Westerfield had dry-cleaned, and her blood was also detected on a sample of the carpeting in his RV.

Ironically, bleach — as detectives Keene and Parga had smelled the first time they went into Westerfield's garage and as was also written at the top of a shopping list investigators later found in his kitchen — will destroy DNA. Despite Westerfield's attempts to rid his belongings of any evidence, he had missed a few spots.

Police had found the smoking gun.

"I can't stress how important that link is," announced Police Chief David Bejarano. But without a body, prosecutors had to settle for charging their suspect with kidnapping.

"We are very happy the police have made an arrest," said Brenda van Dam, bravely speaking to the same reporters who had so recently seemed bent on exposing her ugliest secrets.

"But the fact remains we still don't have our daughter. We still need to find Danielle."

CHAPTER 4

For close to a full month after the night Danielle van Dam vanished from her bed, hundreds of volunteers continued the arduous task of looking for the little girl through the desert terrain around San Diego. Despite the lack of a body, Deputy District Attorney Jeff Dusek, a prosecutor with more than twenty-five years of experience in putting the worst of criminals behind bars, intended to file murder charges against Westerfield. He obviously wouldn't be satisfied with winning merely kidnapping and possession of child pornography convictions.

"I must conclude that Danielle van Dam is no longer living and was killed," the District Attorney, Paul Pfingst, told a news conference. To try someone for murder without a body, the state would have to establish a "reasonable probability" that the victim had died. Pfingst added that he would file a so-called special circumstance — murder during kidnapping — allowing for the death penalty if David Westerfield was found guilty.

Pfingst described an emotional weekend spent with Danielle's parents, saying, "It was difficult to bring out the word 'murder.' Both parents were in tears."

The van Dams were still hoping and praying for their little girl's return.

"They're maintaining their privacy but also want to thank anyone involved in the search," said family spokeswoman Sara Fraunces. "They're just continuing to try to find Danielle."

Recognizing his uphill battle, Westerfield's attorney Steven Feldman promised only "a vigorous defense." The lawyer began to devise a game plan to cast doubt on whether Danielle was, in fact, dead.

Within days, all of that would change.

On Wednesday, February 27, volunteers returned to an area near El Cajon, twenty-five miles east of San Diego, on "a hunch." By a small grove of oak trees, just off a winding, two-lane road, they found little Danielle's nude and badly decomposed body callously dumped among trash. The child was wearing a plastic choker, the same one seen in thousands of "MISSING" posters around the country, and a single Mickey Mouse earring.

The San Diego Union-Tribune reported that the group of volunteers had searched the area for nearly three hours, and some had gone home, exhausted from weeks of their heartbreaking mission. With only five of the original thirteen people left, the body was found at 2:05 p.m. One of the remaining searchers, Shawna Miller, claimed that her sister, missing for sixteen years and feared dead, helped guide her team to Danielle.

"I truly believe she was my angel," Miller told a reporter from the *Union-Tribune*, as she barely contained her tears. Two men in Miller's group, Karsten Heimburger and Christopher Morgan, were the ones who actually made the grizzly discovery. Miller had walked back to her car to review maps when the two men called her cell phone to say they had found a body. Heimburger called 911, and the group waited for police, as they had been instructed to do. If a positive light could be shed on the discovery, Miller claimed that looking for Danielle was therapeutic for her.

"I found a little bit of peace," she admitted. "We were all very elated we found her, but at the same time we found a child no longer breathing."

"They [the van Dams] don't know what happened," said Heimburger, "but they know where their baby girl is."

"Now, at the very least, the family can have some kind of closure," added Jill Ward, a volunteer and neighbor of the van Dams, to the newspaper. "Of course, we all wanted to find her alive. But now, as horrible as this ending is, they will be able to move on."

Staying with official protocol in the face of the obvious, San Diego police Lt. Jim Collins said at the scene, "At this point we cannot positively confirm that it is Danielle." Behind him investigators had closed the road and set up bright searchlights as nightfall set in. "However," he admitted, "we don't have any other young children missing in the county that have been reported. It's a high probability that it is her."

By the next day, an autopsy had been completed by the medical examiner, and through dental records and X rays, the body was positively identified as that of Danielle.

"Tonight we believe that Danielle van Dam's body has been found," District Attorney Pfingst announced to the media with a sad but determined expression on his face. He added that the cause of death could not immediately be determined because of the body's state of decomposition.

Police Chief Bejarano had already informed Danielle's parents of the news. The couple was seen thanking volunteers at an office that had been used as a base for the search, then quietly leaving. They did not speak with reporters.

"They mentioned that Danielle's in good hands now," Bejarano said. "There's a lot of tears and a lot of anger at dealing with the loss of their daughter."

At Creekside Elementary School, where Danielle had been in the second grade, teachers and parents alike attempted to deal with the sorrow. A dozen counselors converged with a brief script that teachers read at the beginning of class: "As you may have heard on the news, the search team yesterday found a body that may be Danielle.

"We are all very sad and concerned at this time . . . "

Parents grappled with how to help children who were still in denial or who were terrified they would be kidnapped next. Counselors suggested that parents listen to their children's fears and talk about them. They told parents not to dwell on the matter and to try to provide a familiar routine, if at all possible. Still, five substitutes filled in for teachers who needed time to themselves.

In one third-grade class, the children were given several minutes to write about Danielle. The children all lowered their heads and recalled their former friend in brief essays.

The annual father/daughter dance, the same one that Danielle had been looking forward to attending, was postponed for a second time. School officials once hoped that Danielle would come home and that she and her father could be at the dance together.

At the site where Danielle's body was found, a makeshift memorial quickly grew.

Strangers, many openly grieving, appeared with flowers, stuffed animals, and ribbons of pink and purple, the little girl's favorite colors. They left behind teddy bears, cards, and even wind chimes. Tied to a tree was a sign written in magic marker: "Danielle, we never knew you, but we will always remember you."

The Reverend Joseph Acton, who had been counseling the

family during their ordeal, described the couple as devastated but strong. "Brenda said today that love conquers evil."

Little did the van Dams know that at the very moment Danielle's body was discovered, Westerfield's attorneys had been trying to broker a plea deal for their client.

The development was learned months later through a report by *The San Diego Union-Tribune*, citing law enforcement sources.

Feldman, now joined by codefense counsel attorney Robert Boyce, was trying to avoid a potential death sentence for Westerfield: The lawyers were discussing the possibility that Westerfield would reveal where Danielle's body had been dumped in exchange for a promise that prosecutors would not seek the death penalty.

"The deal was just minutes away," revealed one of the *Union-Tribune*'s law enforcement sources.

Apparently, Feldman and Boyce had been at the San Diego jail discussing the final arrangements of the plea bargain with Westerfield. When the lawyers went to meet with prosecutors, they saw the media gathering in the street and asked what was going on. After learning that a body had been found, they went directly to the nearby Hall of Justice for their appointment with prosecutors.

According to the *Union-Tribune*, the defense lawyers were handed a copy of a Thomas Guide map of the Dehesa area, on which a circle had been drawn indicating the location of the body. Any and all negotiations for a plea bargain were immediately called off.

CHAPTER 5

A pretrial hearing to determine if enough evidence existed to try David Westerfield for possession of child pornography, kidnapping and murder took place in early March 2002. The prosecution summarily listed for Judge H. Ronald Domnitz additional witnesses and new evidence that went beyond Westerfield's bloodstained jacket and carpet. The defense, meanwhile, tried to shift the focus to the van Dams' "alternative" lifestyle.

So recently encouraged by the discovery of Danielle's body, Deputy District Attorney Jeff Dusek soon realized that his optimism might have been premature. One of the first witnesses called during the pretrial hearing was the medical examiner who performed the autopsy on the little girl.

"A lot of the body was destroyed by animals," Dr. Brian Blackbourne testified. Exposure to wildlife and the elements left the remains decomposed to the point that doctors were unable to determine how she had died or whether she had been sexually assaulted. Blackbourne explained there were no obvious signs of trauma, like gunshot wounds or ligature marks. Added the doctor, "The deterioration of even the tissue that was there makes it difficult to determine a cause of death."

Still, there was some evidence that showed little Danielle's last moments were spent in undeniable pain and horror. Four of her front teeth were gone, and one was found lodged in the back of her throat. The prosecutors were quick to speculate that Westerfield must have violently gagged the young girl, stuffed something into her mouth, or punched her in the face to keep her quiet. That would also explain the small bloodstain on the shoulder of his jacket. An image of an enraged Westerfield hauling the injured Danielle to her death emerged.

Ultimately, Judge Domnitz, as expected by both sides, set jury selection for a trial to begin on May 17, 2002. Judge William Mudd, described by colleagues as a bright, no-nonsense man who was not afraid to speak his mind, would preside over those proceedings.

By June 4, Dusek was addressing the jury in San Diego Supreme Court with his opening remarks. The prosecutor, while looking into the eyes of the six men and six women, urged them to consider only the young victim and her killer. Westerfield, after having his evil way with the girl, dumped her body just three miles from the Sycuan Casino where he was a member of the slot club. Although no one saw him at the club, it was a crowded place where someone could have come and gone without attracting too much attention. By the end of the trial, with the help of extensive forensic evidence, they would be able to determine without question that Westerfield had killed little Danielle. It fell to the jurors to see that justice was done.

As the lights were turned off and the room went dark, a projector flashed a school photo of Danielle alongside a mug shot of Westerfield onto the wall. Dusek announced, "This trial will be about two people . . . David Westerfield and what he did to Danielle van Dam."

To some degree, Dusek was trying to offset what he knew from the pretrial hearing was coming. When Feldman rose for his turn with the jurors, the defense attorney immediately urged the panel to consider not the victim and her accused attacker but the sex lives and substance abuse of her parents and their friends. With a rapid-fire address, he described Brenda and Damon van Dam as more concerned with getting high and their next "swingers date" than with the safety of their own children. The neglectful parents brought all kinds of questionable people into their home, he maintained.

Feldman's strategy was harsh and abrasive, but as he and his cocounsel, Robert Boyce, saw it, they had to try whatever they could to raise reasonable doubt in jurors' minds. Experts in defense, commenting to the media, who were as infatuated with this proceeding as they had been with the crime itself, agreed that if Feldman didn't pursue the lifestyle issue, he would be doing his client a disservice. Others suggested that the attorney must have known that San Diego jury members, traditionally more conservative than those in other urban areas, were prime candidates to be offended by drug use or free sex.

Also, despite the seasoned defense attorney's efforts to dismiss the prosecution's evidence as merely circumstantial, Feldman must have known Westerfield's odds for an acquittal were slim at best. The jury had already gasped at samples of the defendant's porn collection and leaned forward in their seats when told how investigators found binoculars in his bathroom next to a window screen that had been bent outward so he could spy directly into Danielle's bedroom. Despite running the risk of alienating jurors, Feldman knew his best chance may have been to try to divert the focus.

"Brenda is putting the moves on people, meaning she's

behaving in a sexually aggressive manner," Feldman said, describing the girls' night out at Dad's Café on the evening Danielle vanished. "Brenda was trying to bring company home to Damon . . . Interesting as to who they allow in their door."

Despite Feldman's implications that any number of potential killers had traipsed through the van Dam household, one image stuck in the minds of everyone present in the courtroom that first day.

"What did you see?" Dusek asked volunteer Karsten Heimburger, the same man who had spoken to *The San Diego Union-Tribune* regarding the moment his search party stumbled upon the trash-strewn dump site.

"Danielle's body," he answered, noticeably shaken. "The body was laying down on her back. Her head was facing to her right."

Over the next two days, the prosecution called Brenda and Damon van Dam to testify. If the defense intended to discredit the parents, Dusek would get that over with, then conclude his case with the irrefutable hard evidence. He also hoped to show the van Dams not as swingers, but as good parents who never deserved to lose their beloved daughter.

The van Dams had initially shied away from the courtroom during some of the most graphic pretrial testimony. The medical examiner had described the "mummified" state of Danielle's body, including how the little girl's hands had to be removed and "rehydrated" to obtain fingerprints. That was too much for them to hear, but now they were prepared to face Westerfield. Their daughter had been murdered, and they needed to make sure the man who violently took her would never hurt another little girl.

With Dusek's prodding, Damon van Dam speculated about his daughter's abduction from the safety of her bedroom. The father, choking back tears, showed jurors photographs of Danielle's room, pointing out various dolls and favorite toys. He admitted that he and his wife would never be the same after such a loss.

On cross-examination, Feldman, just as Dusek expected, asked Damon only about his lifestyle. Although the prosecutor had befriended the van Dams during their ordeal, there was nothing Dusek could do now but sit back and watch. Flushed and noticeably embarrassed, van Dam confirmed that he had had sex with other women while his wife watched. He added, "I have opened my life up, every detail, to try to get my daughter back and now to get justice for her."

But the stressful questioning was taking its toll. Later, Damon stared at supporters in the gallery in utter frustration and then slammed his forehead down onto the witness box.

Brenda van Dam took the stand looking nervous and pale, and she immediately broke down when Dusek asked her how many children she had.

"Three," she managed to reply while dabbing tears with a tissue. She then named Derrick, Dylen, and also Danielle before commenting that the youngest, Dylen, was celebrating his sixth birthday that day. She later sobbed uncontrollably after glancing at photos of Danielle's room.

In turn, Feldman predictably asked Brenda van Dam about her lifestyle. She admitted that on one occasion in October 2000, she and her husband had sex with another couple and a woman. Two of the participants were Barbara Easton and Denise Kemal, the same friends who were with her at Dad's Café the night Danielle vanished. "And with regards to those women, both you and your husband have engaged in sex with them and their male partners?" asked Feldman.

"Yes," replied Brenda, before adding, "I would have told them [the police] anything they asked to get

Danielle back. None of this matters."

It was apparent the jury was beginning to agree with Brenda on that point. As Feldman posed uncomfortable question after uncomfortable question to the van Dams, few jurors took notes. Some even noticeably stared at the lawyer rather than at the parents as they struggled with their answers.

Called to testify about that fateful evening at Dad's Café, Denise Kemal became an obvious highlight for the jurors rather than the despicable character Feldman portrayed her as being. The panel leaned out from their box to see Kemal enter the court, and they laughed as the petite brunette spoke in a soft voice and giggled throughout the less serious parts of her testimony. It appeared that Feldman's strategy was pushing the jurors to sympathize with the van Dams and their friends rather than condemn them as the defense attorney had hoped.

Over the course of the next few days, Dusek proceeded to call various witnesses who attested to Westerfield's "strange behavior" after Danielle disappeared. They included Detectives Keene and Parga, as well as the neighbor, Christina Hoeffs, who had seen Westerfield's home oddly "locked down" at 2 a.m. the night of the abduction. Hoeffs now recalled another peculiar fact beyond what she initially told investigators: Westerfield always prepared his RV for hours before departing on a trip. That morning, he was gone when the sun came up.

Westerfield had admitted to Detectives Keene and Parga that his RV had gotten stuck in the desert sand, resulting in the many abrasions on his hands from trying to dig himself out. Investigators had found the tow-truck driver who eventually came to his aid. Apparently, the man, Dan Conklin, heard an unidentified third voice while he was assisting Westerfield with the RV. The site was remote, and besides Westerfield and himself, there were no other campers around.

"I thought I heard someone say something," said Conklin.

"Did you think you two were alone?" asked Dusek.

"Yes."

Westerfield had also claimed he had lost his wallet to account for some of his random travels as he tried to find it. Prosecutors produced a park volunteer who contested that argument. Donald Raymond, a volunteer at the Silver Strand State Beach Park who deals with collecting fees, said he personally saw that missing wallet on the morning in question. Westerfield "pulled out his wallet and showed me three or four $20 bills" when the two discussed his bill, said Raymond.

Others at the campground also testified about seeing Westerfield the Saturday morning that Brenda first realized Danielle was missing. Beverly Askey, at Silver Strand with friends, said that no sooner had Westerfield parked, he closed the curtain on the front dashboard. All of his windows were blocked, preventing anyone from seeing inside.

Joyce Rodgers, parked in a nearby RV, also watched Westerfield pull into the lot Saturday morning between 10 and 11 a.m. and wondered about the same thing. She said to the court, "Everyone we know that drives a motor home leaves the windows open.

"It was so unusual," Rodgers explained, that she and her son-in-law began wondering if "maybe he had a girlfriend."

CHAPTER 6

Slowly but surely, lead prosecutor Jeff Dusek was poking holes in Westerfield's already shaky alibi. With calculated precision, he had saved the best of his witnesses for last. The most damning evidence against Westerfield, as promised in opening arguments, would come from a myriad of forensic scientists.

"Forensic" simply means "pertaining to, or involved with, a court of law." There are, among other forensic scientists, fingerprint experts, hair experts, DNA experts, and fiber experts, all of which Dusek would now call to testify. Despite their varied specialties, all shared the same goal — to indisputably link Danielle van Dam's murder to David Westerfield.

One of the first forensic scientists at the crime scene was Karen LeAlcala, an expert in human hair analysis. Her background included two years of classes on "evidence technology" from Grossmont College in El Cajon, coincidentally the same town where Danielle's body had been found. After graduation, LeAlcala endured a rigorous training program with the SDPD before going into her present field.

Hair analysis is one of the least exact of the forensic sciences, its findings marked by "consistencies" and "probabilities." It includes the painstaking retrieval of samples that are compared with others under high-powered microscopes in the hope of finding a match.

Dusek began the questioning by asking LeAlcala about the things she saw and found when she first arrived at the scene. "Can you tell us broadly what they include?" he asked.

LeAlcala listed towels, pillow shams, and bedding in Westerfield's laundry in the garage. Dryer lint, a bleach bottle, and other discarded items were also all bagged and labeled.

"Anything else?" Dusek asked, referring to the rest of the house.

"I collected video cassette tapes and a bottle of what was labeled as I.D. Juicy Lube in the bedroom."

"If you could, are there any photographs on exhibit 46 that demonstrate the location of — I'm sorry, you said 'bottle of Juicy Lube'?"

"Yes," the witness said, pointing to a photograph. "You can see it best where item number 8 is."

"Just for the record," Dusek turned to the jurors, "you've pointed to a photograph in exhibit 107, slightly to the right of center, which appears to be either in or against the headboard [of Westerfield's bed] with the sign 'number 8.' Is that correct?"

"Correct."

After craftily setting the scene of Westerfield's bedroom as a well-equipped lair for lewd sex, Dusek had the witness reveal the hard evidence, the kind she had been officially trained to find. In the laundry lint a human hair "consistent" with that of Danielle van Dam had been recovered. The witness confirmed it had likely come from the bedding Westerfield was washing.

After recounting how LeAlcala then moved on to Westerfield's Southwinds motor home and particularly into its bathroom, Dusek asked, "Did you find something in that sink? Did you find any human hairs?"

"Yes."

"Can you tell us about that?"

"I did collect hair from the bathroom sink basin drain with a pair of tweezers."

As Dusek knew, that hair had eventually also been found to be consistent with Danielle van Dam's. More important, the length of that hair was eight inches, lending to Dusek's argument that it had to have been left *after* Danielle received a haircut only a few days before she disappeared.

Defense attorney Feldman had continually tried to discount any forensic link to Danielle found in the RV, arguing that neighborhood kids often snuck into Westerfield's RV "to play" when it was parked on the street. Suddenly, an open-ended window of time shortened — Danielle had to have been "playing" in the bathroom of the RV within the last few days before her death.

Feldman, during his turn with the witness, attempted to refute the accuracy of hair analysis. LeAlcala admitted that she could definitively say only that the hair was "from one of the van Dams," but she argued that Danielle's two brothers and father had short hair, and Brenda's was long. Only the little victim's was dirty blonde and eight inches long.

Next, Dusek called Jeffrey Graham, a fingerprint analyst. Graham had tirelessly lifted more than three hundred fingerprints from the van Dams' home. Through a process that included first finding the nearly invisible clues by dusting a black powder on doorknobs, tables, and banisters, the expert then matched those against a computerized database by examining the ridges, creases, and points of the prints. Graham eventually identified a total of 122 out of those original 300 from the van Dams' home, but none belonged to Westerfield.

After conducting the same exhaustive exercise on Westerfield's RV, Graham discovered only two prints. The vehicle had obviously been thoroughly cleaned, as prosecutors immediately pointed out. Still, minute evidence was missed in the cleaning, and Graham managed to find it. The two prints matched Danielle van Dam's.

"A damp rag will wipe it right off," Graham explained, regarding the fragility of any print, left by the oils that accumulate on the skin. "Even casual brushing will wipe it off."

Graham testified, more specifically, that Danielle had left a print from her left hand on a cabinet, about a foot above the bed's headboard. Two fingers in particular — the ring and middle fingers — were clear.

"How certain are you?" asked Dusek.

"Absolutely certain," replied Graham.

The best Feldman could come up with to refute the newest testimony was to assert again that neighborhood kids often snuck into Westerfield's RV. The expert didn't, after all, know *how* the print got onto the cabinet.

Annette Peer of the San Diego Police Department's crime lab is a DNA expert. DNA, which stands for deoxyribonucleic acid, is the genetic material contained in cells. All organic matter contains a highly specific DNA sequence, which, when analyzed, is converted into a computerized image resembling a supermarket bar code. Danielle van Dam's bar code had been positively identified on Westerfield's jacket and on a section of carpeting taken from his RV, between a closet and the bathroom.

This undeniable link was illustrated by the expert's

figures: There was only a 1 in 670 quadrillion chance the blood on the jacket came from someone else and only a 1 in 130 quadrillion chance the blood on the carpet stain was not Danielle's. Peer explained that a quadrillion is a 1 followed by fifteen zeroes. The entire world's population is 6 billion, or a 6 followed by nine zeros.

Feldman, for the time being, was left with no theory to counter this evidence. Earlier, besides his well-used theory of neighborhood kids sneaking into and playing in Westerfield's RV, he had asserted that any additional forensic link between Danielle and Westerfield could have come from the time his client bought Girl Scout cookies from the little girl, or when he and Brenda talked at Dad's Café. Now that comment seemed almost insulting to jurors.

Finally, the prosecution called Jennifer Shen, a fiber analyst. The meticulous process of fiber analysis requires investigators to comb through objects with a microscope. They search for tiny out-of-place fibers that may have fallen from clothing, carpeting, or other kinds of fabric. Criminalists then use more powerful microscopes to look for traits specific to the manufacturing process and run the fibers through a battery of chemical tests meant to identify the type of material and the dyes used to color it.

As Shen testified, an orange acrylic fiber was abundant in defendant David Westerfield's home but showed up only once on the victim — wrapped between the links of the plastic choker that was still on her neck when she was found. Despite the state of the body, another clue had been found.

"The long, bright orange fibers were significant to me because I had seen a bright orange fiber somewhere else and that triggered my memory," said Shen. "Tangled in hair that was tangled around the necklace was a long, orange fiber."

Specifically, Shen told the court that the fiber from Danielle's necklace matched 20 to 30 fibers found in

Westerfield's washer, 50 to 100 found on top of the washer, another 50 to 100 found in his laundry, and 10 to 20 found in the bedding in his master bedroom.

Adding to the testimony, another police expert, Melvyn Kong, who also specializes in trace evidence, noted that none of the fibers found in the van Dams' bedding and home matched the orange acrylic fiber Shen discovered in the choker.

What all of this meant was that the orange fiber found in Danielle's necklace on her decomposed body did not come from Danielle's own home, but rather from Westerfield's. Therefore, the little girl most likely had to have been in Westerfield's home just prior to her murder.

In yet another link, Shen disclosed that a microscopic purple fiber from the rug in Danielle's room was found on the floor of David Westerfield's RV. Now, in addition to the orange fiber placing the little girl in Westerfield's home just prior to her murder, it appeared that Westerfield could have been in Danielle's room. He may have picked up the purple fiber on his clothes or shoes while abducting the girl and then tracked it back to his RV.

Up to this point in the trial, Feldman had been left to merely cross-examine the prosecution's witnesses. By early July, it was his turn to call people to testify. He produced an expert to back his theory that the fiber evidence may have been transferred to or from his client when Westerfield spoke with Brenda van Dam that night at Dad's Café. Next came a computer expert who asserted the huge library of pornography that had been found could have belonged to Westerfield's son, who often used his father's computer. Then, in a shrewd move to further counter the hair, fingerprint, DNA, and fiber evidence against his client, Feldman would bring his own forensic scientist, an entomologist, or bug expert, to the stand.

The use of entomology in courts can be traced back to thirteenth-century China and has gradually gained acceptance in American courtrooms over the last twenty years. There are only a few certified forensic entomologists in North America. By studying the presence of flies, maggots, and beetles at a crime scene, entomologists can obtain estimates regarding a time a victim may have died.

David Faulkner, in graphic testimony, described his findings after attending the autopsy. He told jurors that insects first infested Danielle's corpse between February 8 and 16. Infestation can begin immediately after a dead body is dumped. The relevance of this new data raised doubts of when, in fact, the little girl had been killed.

Prosecutors had implied that Westerfield killed Danielle and disposed of her body between February 2 and 4, before investigators began tailing him. By February 5, Westerfield rarely left their watchful eyes. It would have been impossible for him to dump the body in its final remote location after that date. Still, Faulkner asserted, "None of the maggots I looked at" indicated that Danielle was left outside before February 4. In addition, the witness noted that "whatever flies were in the area" should have been instantly drawn to the body, and he found no evidence that they were present before February 16.

Dusek, so recently on the offensive, was left to argue that "extremely abnormal" temperatures in San Diego could have skewed Faulkner's conclusions during that period. Insect life can depend on many variables at a crime scene, including temperature and precipitation. Faulkner acknowledged that the record-setting heat and lack of rain had severely diminished the number of flies. In fact, Faulkner admitted he had never seen fewer flies in the area than that February.

Even so, it was a major win for Feldman. Faulkner had initially become involved when he was hired by the prosecution to help their own case, and the medical examiner had willingly invited him to attend the autopsy. All parties believed he would come to a conclusion indicating Westerfield's guilt. Now Faulkner had presented the strongest evidence yet for the defense.

CHAPTER 7

After nearly three brutal months, it came time for closing arguments on Tuesday, August 6, 2002. The courtroom was packed, as it had been every day for the trial. Dusek, once again looking into the eyes of the jurors, called the murder of Danielle van Dam an "evil, evil crime" and urged jurors to convict David Westerfield on all charges.

"He's guilty of these crimes. He's guilty of the ultimate evil. He's guilty to the core," Dusek announced while shouting and pointing a finger at the defense table. The child pornography revealed a motive: Westerfield was a homicidal sex addict — infatuated with sick fantasies involving prepubescent girls.

"He gives us a bogus story that just doesn't wash," said Dusek, referring to Westerfield's account of his whereabouts on the weekend that Danielle was abducted. Instead of spending an innocent weekend in his RV, Dusek argued Westerfield passed that time "having his way" with Danielle before killing her.

At one point, Dusek slammed his hand down onto

the jury box rail to simulate Danielle's head "striking Westerfield's headboard as he raped her," sending Brenda van Dam running toward the exit in tears.

Then, according to the prosecutor, Westerfield searched for a place to dump her body "like any other trash."

"All the sex, the alcohol, who's doing this, who's doing that. That's got nothing to do with her kidnapping," Dusek continued before listing other potential suspects the defense wanted the jurors to consider, including "the bogeyman."

Regarding Feldman's entomologist, Dusek said, "Everyone's different, has a different estimation, approximation, some might even say guess. This [entomology] is not an exact science. This is *not* DNA."

Holding up an autopsy photo of Danielle's badly decomposed corpse, Dusek then recounted all the forensic evidence he had provided. By all estimates, even the least exact — hair analysis — was more accurate than entomology. The hair, the fingerprints, and the DNA came from the body itself.

"From Danielle herself," he added, "she helps to solve this case . . . Proof beyond a reasonable doubt? Proof beyond a *possible* doubt."

Westerfield, as he had for most of the trial, gazed stone-faced and straight ahead during the prosecutor's closing arguments. Damon van Dam, his wife now out in the hall, stared at the floor. The jurors, having hung on Dusek's every word, watched as the prosecutor returned to his seat.

Once again the defense had their turn. Where Dusek had systematically recounted his case from memory, Feldman raced around the well of the court while sifting through papers, sitting in the witness chair to make a point, even struggling to display large posterboards of photos by balancing them on his arm or propping them against his face.

Feldman first argued that the person who took Danielle van Dam from her bed and murdered her was not David Westerfield but someone the little girl knew and trusted, explaining, "The only thing that's logical is that when she woke up, she knew the person in there." Otherwise, he said, the second-grader would have screamed "bloody murder."

Regarding the bloodstains found in his client's RV and on his jacket, Feldman said, "I want to know how that blood got there." Then, pointing to the jury, he added, "You have a right to know."

Expanding on his theory that Danielle must have sneaked into the RV to play, Feldman simply suggested, "Kids bleed all the time."

He pointed out there was no evidence, "not hair, not fingerprints, not fiber, not nothing" showing that Westerfield had been in the van Dam house. The many unidentified fingerprints in their home, prints determined not to belong to the defendant, pointed to some other perpetrator. That "mystery man" was most likely someone brought in to contact with Danielle through her parents' unconventional sex life.

Several times during the argument, Judge William Mudd interrupted Feldman's argument to correct him. At one point, when Feldman said the prosecution's theory was that Danielle was killed in her bed, Mudd said, "That completely misstates the evidence."

Even so, Feldman concluded, "The evidence has been introduced that Mr. Westerfield is not guilty. There it is."

On Thursday, August 8, just after 1 p.m., the panel of six

men and six women rose from their seats, gathered purses, water bottles, and notepads, then silently departed for another room. It now fell to them to deliberate murder, kidnapping, and child pornography charges in the slaying of Danielle van Dam. Considering Dusek's early filing of "murder under special circumstances," they all knew that their verdict could potentially carry the death penalty for Westerfield.

As hours turned into days, speculation ran rampant among the media concerning which way the jury might be leaning. Legal experts weighed in on both sides of the debate. Some claimed the delay was a positive sign for Westerfield, that despite all the forensic evidence, Feldman had succeeded in instilling reasonable doubt. Others argued that the passing days were only indicative of a jury recognizing the gravity of their impending decision. Then there were those who predicted a deadlock, which could result in an entirely new trial.

Finally, on Wednesday, August 21, their tenth day of deliberations, the jury announced just after 1 p.m. that they had reached a verdict. In the hushed courtroom, observers could have heard a pin drop after the foreman was asked by the judge to announce that verdict aloud.

With a hard expression on his face, the foreman, who happened to be a new father, replied, "Guilty."

"Oh my God!" exclaimed Brenda van Dam, her trembling hands covering her mouth. Damon wrapped his arms around her, and they both began to cry tears of relief. Westerfield's sister, sitting with her husband in the second row of the gallery, wept behind dark sunglasses, shaking her head in disbelief. David Westerfield showed no emotion.

Outside the San Diego Supreme Court, a crowd that had assembled broke into cheers.

Once a defendant has been found guilty of murder under special circumstances in the state of California, sentencing falls to the jury in a separate vote. Their choices for Westerfield were life in prison or death. During this final stage, known as the penalty phase, any new evidence can be provided.

Dusek immediately produced Westerfield's niece, now a college student, who recalled that when she was seven years old, her uncle snuck into her room. The witness, identified only as Jenny N. to protect her privacy, testified, "My Uncle Dave had his fingers in my mouth and he was kinda playing with my teeth." After initially pretending to be asleep, "I bit him really hard for as long as I could," when he put his finger in her mouth again.

According to Jenny N., Westerfield fled the room, but only after he "readjusted" his running shorts.

Westerfield himself had led investigators to Jenny N., telling them in one of his initial interviews that there had been a "misunderstanding" in his past after his niece ran straight to her parents following the incident and they confronted him. Now his free admission threatened to seal his fate.

Feldman, his job having taken on new weight, paraded character witness after character witness, all of whom painted a picture of Westerfield as a responsible man with "strong family values."

As with the original deliberations, the jury spent over a week sequestered before emerging on Monday, September 16, with their decision. The same foreman who had pronounced Westerfield guilty on the murder charges now recommended that he be sentenced to death.

CHAPTER 8

Even as the trial ended, no one who had known Westerfield would ever suggest that the roots of his pedophilia and murderous act could be traced to a traumatic or abusive upbringing, which is a common thread in the lives of many vicious killers. By all accounts, David Alan Westerfield had an idyllic childhood.

He was born in 1952 to David Horatio Westerfield and his wife, Laura. Just as his dad was called by his middle name, Horatio, young David was called Alan by his family. Two siblings followed, Earl and then Tania. The children's youth was spent on a farm in rural Maine where their father, a respected member of the community, served in the state legislature in the early 1960s. Their mother was a contented housewife, doting on the kids' every need.

"We had a very nice childhood in my opinion," Tania would recount in a hushed courtroom on August 29, 2002, during the penalty phase of the trial. She was, by this point, pleading with the jury to spare her brother from the death penalty after he had been convicted of killing Danielle.

As Tania recalled, her and her brothers' upbringing was

free of trauma. Their parents never fought, nor were the kids ever physically abused or molested by anyone. There was no alcoholism or drug abuse in the family, they were not poor, and they took "fun vacations" and attended good schools. Their mom was always there for them.

"We lived on a farm, in my great-grandmother's home, which we took care of for her. And during the summers we would water-ski. We owned an island in the middle of a freshwater lake in Maine. It had two cottages on it, so some of the summers we would stay on the island. There was no running water and electricity. It was kind of like camping."

The Maine winters meant more fun for young David and his siblings — snow skiing and ice skating atop a pond on their farm that froze early most years.

"It was a very nice childhood," Tania repeated.

A strong work ethic was part of the Westerfield family culture. As David approached his teens, he took on summer jobs, including serving as a lifeguard at a national park on St. George's Lake. He also gathered wild blueberries from the Maine hillsides, a backbreaking job that required crouching and dragging a short-handled metal rake over the ground-level crop to pull the tiny berries from the bushes.

While most of Westerfield's childhood was spent in Maine, there was a short stint in the early 1960s when Horatio took the family to San Diego so he could enroll in art classes at San Diego State University. They returned to Maine after that, but in 1967, Horatio decided to move the family west for good, having acquired a taste for Southern California's warm and sunny climate.

Soon the family settled into their new lifestyle in the Clairemont section of San Diego. Horatio took the family on frequent car trips to the desert where they explored dry riverbeds and sand dunes. Holidays were spent at Horatio's mother's home in Point Loma. Horatio and Laura started their own typesetting and graphics business, printing matchbooks and even a legal magazine called *Dicta*.

David, now an ambitious student at Madison High School, took on after-school and summer jobs during his junior and senior years, washing dishes at a restaurant in Mission Beach and working at a local Ramada Inn motel.

In a senior-year physics class, David met Margaret Hennon. Sparks flew and soon they began dating. "He was my first serious sweetheart," said Hennon, who thirty years later still cherishes a pair of earrings he gave her during the romance. Hennon wore those earrings to court when she, like David's sister, Tania, testified on his behalf.

Hennon explained that their courtship could be characterized by romantic drives around San Diego and Del Mar admiring the landscape and architecture. They became so close, "He called my mother 'mom.' He was a member of the family," said Hennon, who at various times smiled at Westerfield or cried on the witness stand as she recounted her fond memories of the courtship.

Westerfield had taken Hennon to museums, plays, and the senior prom. He even proposed to her, although they never married. Noticeably absent during her testimony was any explanation as to why the romance ended. But although she had not spoken to him in twenty years, when she heard he was charged with Danielle van Dam's murder, she sent him an emotional greeting card offering to help him "in any way I can." The David she knew would never hurt a child, much less kill one.

Yet for such a supportive home environment and pleasant childhood, both David and his younger brother, Earl, were in a hurry to leave at the first possible opportunity. "David moved out when he was eighteen, right out of high school. He went to a junior college in Mesa and worked. And then when Earl turned eighteen, he moved out . . . and down the line they were roommates together," Tania recounted.

Were the Westerfield brothers just fiercely independent, anxious to set out and make their mark on the world? Or was there something unpleasant pushing them out the door of their parents' house, something Tania did not know or would not reveal? Were there family secrets?

The unexpected bad news that came in 1974, as Tania was approaching her high school graduation, shook the Westerfield children to the core. Their parents, Horatio and Laura, announced they were splitting up.

"We were all kind of shocked about it," recalled Tania. "My parents never argued in front of us, never disputed anything. They always seemed to get along, so we were kind of set back by the thing."

David, then twenty-two, was upset and wondered about his future. Later in life, when he had kids of his own, where would he take them at Christmas? To Mom's or Dad's? Tania went on, "He wanted a traditional family life. He wanted his kids to be able to go to their grandparents' house."

Ironically, some years later, David himself would divorce after a long, seemingly happy marriage. During the early 1970s, David had been married briefly to a woman named Debbie. Despite the swift ending of that relationship, David met a new woman named Jackie in the mid '70s, and they tied the knot in 1979 and stayed together for seventeen years.

On the outside, things seemed fine. The Westerfields had two kids, Lisa and Neal, whom they adored. Both parents enjoyed entertaining at home, especially having barbecues by the pool. There were family camping trips. They appeared content. Then Jackie decided to end it, initiating a divorce. By all accounts from the couple's close friends and family, both she and David apparently decided to keep the reason to themselves.

Tania testified that David was upset about his divorce and

still loved Jackie at that time. But when prosecutor Jeff Dusek asked her if she knew why the marriage ended, it was Westerfield's defense lawyer, Steven Feldman, who objected and prevented her from answering. Perhaps he feared an unexpected disclosure that might open those doors he was trying to keep closed, and he wanted to keep the parade of praise coming.

Susan Lelek, a girlfriend of Westerfield's after his divorce from Jackie, praised him as a kind man who helped set up hospice care for her dying father. He later consoled the family and helped make funeral arrangements when her dad succumbed to liver cancer.

Lelek also recalled how a bighearted Westerfield took in her daughter Christina and her one-year-old son when the young woman fled an abusive relationship. He also helped Susan buy an SUV when she needed a new car, and he was always "very generous" with money. "I still care about him," she said and then broke down crying when asked to recall the last time she had seen him in person. Through tears she answered, "Three weeks prior to the time he was arrested." They had broken up just before Danielle van Dam's abduction.

The Millers were neighbors from Treeridge Terrace where David and Jackie Westerfield lived during much of their marriage. They glowingly described him as a dear and trusted friend who watered their lawn and swept their patio when they were away. Alden and Kathleen Miller told of many fun-filled times when their family played Pictionary or Trivial Pursuit with the Westerfields, and they all attended one another's birthdays and holiday functions. He even counseled their kids.

The Millers' oldest son, Michael, now a lawyer, said of Westerfield, "He's one of those people who helped me get where I am today." He also described him as "a mentor."

A band of Westerfield's professional colleagues also testified to his great talents as a designer of medical rehabilitation devices, including prosthetic knuckle implants and a knee rehabilitation device.

"I would guess it's been used by millions," said orthopedic surgeon Richard Coutts, who conceived the device and worked with Westerfield to develop it.

Ironically, for months on end during the trial, Westerfield sat stone-faced while the most gruesome details of Danielle's murder and the ravaged condition of her corpse were described. He never once choked up when Brenda van Dam sobbed at the horrors, sometimes doubled over in her grief.

But Westerfield's eyes filled with tears when Michael Miller, Margaret Hennon, his sister, Tania, and the final witnesses, his children, Lisa and Neal, testified of their devotion to him. Only this moved David Westerfield.

"Still love your father?" defense lawyer Steven Feldman asked Lisa Westerfield.

"Yes," she answered, her voice cracking. Asked if she missed her dad, the college student with shoulder-length auburn hair, replied, "Yes." Describing the many good times spent with her dad and brother, she added, "He took us to the park and hit ground balls to us."

Neal, a college sophomore, had fond memories, too. Asked what he recalled most about his dad, he replied, "Probably laying out by the pool playing chess."

"It matters to you what happens to your father here?" Feldman asked.

"Yes."

CHAPTER 9

Despite the picture of David Westerfield as a favorite neighbor and doting parent, this same man had been convicted of a heinous crime: killing Danielle van Dam. Prosecutors had argued convincingly that this "mentor," this father who "hit ground balls" to his kids and impressed colleagues, also brutally raped a seven-year-old girl, knocked out her teeth, and then dumped her lifeless body in the desert.

For all the people who learned firsthand that Westerfield had a dark side, the family members and friends of Danielle's whose own lives were now permanently scarred with pain and sorrow, came an ultimate question: When and what exactly drove the perfect man to become the most evil of monsters?

It was a warm evening in the early 1990s, and burgers sizzled on the grill as David and Jackie Westerfield sipped drinks and chatted with their guests, a friendly mix of family and neighbors gathered at the couple's spacious home on Treeridge Terrace. The kids darted around the beautifully landscaped yard like fireflies, shrieking joyfully as they played. The air was tinged with barbecue smoke and filled with the hearty laughter that was typical of the get-togethers the Westerfields often hosted during those years.

The couple, it seemed, lived the sun-drenched California dream. They owned a sprawling custom-built home, complete with a swimming pool, a backyard aviary, and even a game room with a pool table, located in the affluent San Diego suburb of Poway. David, a talented engineer, designed innovative medical devices and made very good money. They had two bright and beautiful kids. Lisa, born in 1981, was a natural athlete who loved swimming and soccer. Neal, two years younger, had a great ear for music and played the saxophone. Life was pretty darn good.

On this night, the Westerfields' crowd of revelers included Jackie's older brother, John, his wife, Jeanne, and their two young daughters, Jenny Lynn, born in 1983, and her little sister, who was three years younger. As the partying progressed, David Westerfield hoisted a few glasses of his favorite drink, rum and Coke. He worked hard and enjoyed a cocktail now and then.

The kids were tuckered out long before the adults were ready to call it a night. At nine o'clock, Jackie and Jeanne took the youngsters upstairs. Jeanne tucked her daughters, blonde-haired Jenny Lynn and her sister, into cozy makeshift bedding on the floor. Their cousin, Lisa, settled into her own bed nearby. Left alone, the girls soon drifted off to sleep.

But only an hour later, something woke Jenny Lynn from her hazy slumber. Something very strange was happening in the darkness on the floor at the foot of cousin Lisa's bed — something creepy that made no sense to Jenny Lynn but scared her tremendously.

Her uncle David Westerfield was crouched down beside her with his fingers in her mouth, rubbing her teeth. The frightened and bewildered girl pretended to be asleep because, as she would recount years later, "I was too freaked out about it. I didn't understand what was going on."

As Jenny lay there motionless, Uncle Dave then moved away, going over to Jenny's little sister, who was sleeping soundly next to her. Jenny carefully rolled over and peeked to see what Uncle Dave was doing, but whatever she saw, if anything, didn't stick in her memory.

Soon Uncle Dave came back to Jenny, again sticking his fingers in her mouth. But this time, the frightened girl's adrenaline kicked in, and she bit her uncle as hard as she possibly could.

Westerfield jumped back from the bed, and without saying a word, he walked away from his niece and headed to his daughter Lisa's bedside, where Jenny saw him "adjusting the sides" of his dark-colored running shorts. Then, finally, Uncle Dave left the room.

In the darkness, huddled beneath the blankets, Jenny waited to make sure he was gone. At eleven o'clock, she summoned the courage to go downstairs, where the adults were still partying, and told her mother what had happened. A tearful Jenny simply said, "Uncle Dave was in the room and he was being weird and he bothered me."

Jeanne was nobody's fool. Even without details, the alarm bells were sounding in her head. After calming her daughter and putting her back to bed, Jeanne sought out and confronted her brother-in-law.

David Westerfield had a plausible explanation all figured out.

"He said Jenny had been fussing in her sleep and he was comforting her. It seemed like a reasonable explanation. I didn't question it further," Jeanne later recounted.

Within the family, the incident was buried that night. The good life went on, and the Westerfields and their inlaws continued to socialize. To the knowledge of his family and friends, that was the only such incident ever to occur.

Ironically, the next time the unpleasant episode was discussed, about a decade later, it came from the lips of David Westerfield himself, as he sat in a police interrogation room on February 4, 2002.

Life was not so good anymore. A lot had gone down since the fun-filled barbecue days on Treeridge Terrace. Westerfield and his wife had mysteriously divorced in 1996, and their dream home in Poway was sold in the settlement. And his subsequent love life had been rocky, culminating in the January 2002 break-up with girlfriend Susan Lelek, who'd been his on-again, off-again lover during the previous four years.

Now the fifty-year-old father of two was in the hot seat, being questioned by cops in connection with the disappearance of seven-year-old Danielle van Dam, a bubbly second-grader who lived two doors down from his new home in Sabre Springs, another upscale San Diego suburb located just a few miles from his former home in Poway.

San Diego Police Detective Paul Redden, an interrogation specialist, had asked Westerfield if there was any reason people might suspect him in Danielle's disappearance. To the cop's astonishment, Westerfield recalled the night his sister-in-law confronted him about his visit to Jenny's bed.

"She felt I had molested her children. I felt really bad about it," Westerfield told cops in the tape-recorded interview.

Claiming it was all a misunderstanding, Westerfield said he'd gone into the girls' room after hearing a commotion caused when Jenny's foot got caught in her little sister's pajama leg as the two slept side by side. He told cops he simply separated the girls and went downstairs.

Oddly, Jenny had no recollection of her uncle's fiddling with either her or her sister's pajama legs. Had Uncle Dave done something else before she awoke to find his fingers in her mouth? That would be one of just many horrible questions left to haunt Westerfield's friends and family in the months ahead when he would be charged with and convicted of kidnapping and killing Danielle.

Possibly that moment, that night about a decade earlier, was the first sign — but others would follow.

It's not clear whether Westerfield's drinking was ever an issue in his marriage to Jackie, but it certainly became a problem the year they divorced. In 1996 he was arrested for and convicted of drunk driving. His DMV record also shows he was subsequently involved in two auto accidents, one in Poway in 2000 and another in Oceanside in 2001, although he was not charged with DWI in those cases.

Perhaps the stress and loneliness of the divorce had caused him to drink more heavily. Whatever the reason, boozing continued to be a habit, and it caused trouble in his post divorce romance with Susan Lelek.

At various times during their romance, Susan lived with Westerfield in his home, but she walked out on him three separate times, in part because of his drinking, according to her trial testimony. Lelek revealed that Westerfield became "very quiet" and sometimes "upset" when he drank. And on one occasion when he'd been drinking, he became "forceful," she said, but did not elaborate.

"Basically, you'd see a change in character when he drank?" prosecutor Jeff Dusek asked.

"Yes," Lelek replied.

From the accounts of bar patrons in Dad's Café, where Westerfield had been drinking the night Danielle vanished, and by his own admission, Westerfield was drunk that night.

"I don't remember getting home. That's how bad it was," he told cops who grilled him about Danielle's disappearance. "I was drinking rum and Coke. See, the mistake I made was,

I can handle rum and Coke, but somebody bought me a shot of something. I don't remember what it was."

Drinking the same rum and Cokes he "could handle" had already pushed Westerfield into the bedroom where his niece slept. And now it may have emboldened him to prowl farther from home and find another victim: the neighbors' little girl who had sold him four boxes of Girl Scout cookies a few days earlier. On the night of February 1, 2002, admittedly drunk to the point that he couldn't remember getting home, he snapped, and Danielle van Dam paid the price.

So what fueled Westerfield's sick thoughts during the years between the night he snuck into Jenny's bedroom and then Danielle's? The most obvious answer is what investigators discovered in his home: a vast collection of gruesome child pornography stashed in neatly labeled computer CD-ROMs, Zip drives, and video files.

It's uncertain when exactly Westerfield developed a taste for and began collecting child porn, but a potential timeline emerges from the dated files. Most of the images that cops found were downloaded between 1999 and 2001, court records say.

In all, cops found 64,000 pornographic images on Westerfield's computers, including dozens featuring naked elementary-school girls. Then there was the cartoon that featured a pigtailed girl being violently raped by a grown man. Yet another computer generated video clip featured a girl of eleven or twelve being held down by one man while being raped by another, its audio track featuring the girl's high-pitched frightened wails.

"These are his fantasies," prosecutor Jeff Dusek told jurors at Westerfield's murder trial.

"Someone who watches this kind of violent child pornography is likely to be highly dangerous," explained forensic psychologist Richard Walter, an expert in delving into the thought process of some of the worst criminals in our history. "The rape cartoon would facilitate an elaborate fantasy in the viewer's mind where he would follow the script provided and want to act it out on his own," Walter continued.

"This would be a way for him to satisfy his basest urges. Her every squirm and cry would make him more excited. In his sick mind, he would see the little girl as the aggressor, teasing him and playing hard to get. That way, he could justify doling out the ultimate punishment — death."

In his final argument to jurors at the end of the penalty phase, defense attorney Steven Feldman said the trustworthy friend and dedicated father described by Westerfield's family and friends was not consistent with a murderer.

"You have David Westerfield over here," he said while pointing to his client. "You have a horrible crime over here. The two are not reconcilable."

Prosecutor Jeff Dusek also noted this paradox during his closing arguments as he urged jurors to find Westerfield guilty of capital murder. But Dusek had a different interpretation.

"If Westerfield is the guy, that destroys all our senses of protection. That's the scariest part — he was a normal guy down the street."

Sins of the Father

CHAPTER 10

Oregon City was once a bustling and prosperous lumber town in the Pacific Northwest, its surrounding neighborhoods lined with tall Douglas firs fed by rainy winters. Over the years, more modern businesses and jobs moved elsewhere, leaving 26,000 residents in a town that would become recognized mostly as a working-class Portland suburb. By the beginning of 2002, Oregon City was on the map again, but only for tragic reasons.

On Wednesday, January 9, Ashley Pond, a shy twelve-year-old with straight dark hair and brown eyes, awoke around 7:30 a.m. She began her day like any other, preparing to catch the school bus to Gardiner Middle School. The seventh-grader, standing five-foot-four and weighing only 110 pounds, pulled on a pair of Tommy Hilfiger blue jeans, a sweatshirt, and white Skecher tennis shoes before heading for the kitchen to get some breakfast. As usual, she was running late.

In many ways, Ashley was a typical young girl. She enjoyed music, especially the Backstreet Boys. On her grandfather's karaoke machine, she would sing the old country favorite "Delta Dawn" and the '80s pop song "Manic Monday," but only if there weren't too many people around. She often stayed late after school to practice routines with her dance team, as she had the previous evening, coming home after five o'clock for dinner.

There was, however, a distinctly dark cloud over Ashley's past. The previous fall, Ashley's biological father, Wesley Joseph Roettger Jr., had been charged with sexually abusing his daughter. Apparently, he had been out of the Ponds' life before returning to "spend some time" with Ashley, as he told her mother, Lori. The accusations spanned from March 1996 through December 2000, dating back to when Ashley was only seven, and included some forty felony counts. Among others were ten for first-degree rape and ten more for first-degree sodomy.

As if that weren't enough, although Lori would later describe "typical fights" with Ashley over things like ripped jeans or too much makeup, those fights often brought the local police to their home. The tight apartment Ashley shared with her mother, her mother's fiancé, James Keightley, and two younger sisters, Miranda, age six, and Breanna, eleven, was visited by authorities six times during 2001. The complaints ranged from reports of loud domestic disturbances and drunken parties to the kids being forcibly locked out of their apartment, often left for hours in the hallway.

Urging the police to check for a young girl "about eleven or twelve years old wandering around the parking lot crying," one caller added, "this happens all the time with this family."

If a person could recover from such past and present challenges, Ashley was trying her best. Lately things had been getting better for the family. Lori was five months pregnant by Keightley, a thirty-five-year-old warehouse worker who was Ashley's godfather. The twelve-year-old was admittedly excited about the baby and felt she would have to look after her two younger sisters. She intended to share a room with the newborn and even be there for the delivery.

Demonstrating her new enthusiasm, Ashley had also been doing better in school. She was paying more attention to assignments and her grades were improving, according to teachers. Even some of the same neighbors who had previously called the police were now commenting on how the girl seemed to be coming out of her shell. Despite the family history of sexual and substance abuse, including Lori's arrest for drunk driving in 1998, Ashley was showing potential.

Jacinda McLeod lived in the 125-unit Newell Creek Village Apartments near the Pond family. She told *The Oregonian*, a local paper that would soon rise to the forefront with the *Portland Tribune* in documenting the case, that Ashley had become "a respectful young lady."

That January morning, Lori was half-asleep on the couch when Ashley came out of the kitchen, grabbed her tan backpack, and headed for the door. The two younger girls had already left for school, and Keightley had gone to work.

"Love you, Mom," Ashley said.

"I'll see you tonight," Lori replied as Ashley walked out into the damp forty-degree day without a jacket on at 8 a.m.

The family lived toward the rear of the apartment complex, built on the tip of Newell Creek Canyon, a sprawling area of dense forest that covered hundreds of acres. The complex itself was a cluster of gray two-story buildings with balconies, set back within a deep gully. There were lots of children around, the grounds scattered with bicycles and various toys. Before that day, Newell Creek had been a community where parents felt safe letting their children play outdoors.

That would all change shortly.

Ashley headed up a steep driveway toward South Beavercreek Road, where she had about an eight-minute walk to reach the school bus stop. She never made it there, nor would she ever be seen alive again.

Lori Pond returned from her job as an office manager at an engineering firm around six o'clock that evening. She had no reason to suspect anything was amiss. Gardiner Middle School never notified her of Ashley's absence that day, and it wasn't until 7:19 p.m., after trying to call her daughter's friends and getting nowhere, that Lori dialed the police.

"She's twelve," Lori told the dispatcher. "Ashley would never run away."

By 7:38 p.m., according to Clackamas County dispatch logs, an officer was at the apartment. According to experts in child abductions, the most crucial time in a case such as this are the hours directly after a child is reported missing. Statistics indicate that three-quarters of all kidnapped children who are ultimately killed by an abductor are dead within three hours of being taken. Even so, the officer merely took down a brief report and then left shortly thereafter.

Despite Lori's initial assertion, based on the facts that Ashley had never run away from home before and hadn't packed any clothes, police considered the girl a runaway. Detective Viola Valenzuela-Garcia, assigned the next day to start an investigation, said to *The Oregonian*, "All we had was, she didn't come home from school. We get that frequently." There was no search of the apartment complex that night, and the only person interviewed was Ashley's mother.

There are certain factors police weigh in determining if a child has run away from home. One is age, and Ashley, a soon-to-be teenager, fit into that bracket perfectly. Another factor is whether there has been a family dispute. There had been more than enough evidence from the many police visits to her apartment that the girl's home life, to say the least, was not ideal. There were also no telltale signs of an abduction — no one had seen a thing.

Police Chief Gordon Huiras, in defending the department's slow actions, said that he is reluctant to assume a missing child is abducted because that would require a public appeal. If made too often, such appeals lose their effectiveness. He went on to cite a report that came in shortly after Ashley disappeared, claiming the girl was seen at Clackamas Town Center. Detective Valenzuela-Garcia apparently spent a full day there looking for her.

Regardless, it wasn't until days had passed that the police began to think they might have made a mistake. Despite the fact that the FBI urges local police departments to ask for their help immediately when children disappear, it would be January 18 before Valenzuela-Garcia called them in — a nine-day delay.

Shortly thereafter, nearly two weeks after Ashley disappeared, Oregon City police officers began handing out flyers to a long line of motorists on South Beavercreek Road. Police held up large signs with Ashley's photograph, stared into the faces of drivers, and hoped someone would come forward with a clue.

A search party went through the wooded area surrounding the Newell Creek apartments. But as snow began to fall, Oregon City Detective Gary Harris called off the search shortly after 1 p.m., announcing that they had covered nearly "everything in the area they needed to."

Then the investigation went from cold to frozen.

CHAPTER 11

On Friday, March 8, almost two months to the day after Ashley Pond disappeared without a trace, her thirteen-year-old friend Miranda Gaddis awoke around 7 a.m. and prepared to catch the school bus to Gardiner Middle School. Miranda had straight dark hair and brown eyes, was five-foot-four, weighed only 110 pounds, and lived in the same apartment complex as Ashley. When the two young girlfriends had been seen together, strangers often mistook them as sisters.

After taking a shower, Miranda went into the kitchen wearing a gray terry cloth robe to get some breakfast, her wet hair wrapped in a bath towel. She told her mother, Michelle Duffey, about her upcoming day. School would let out at 1 p.m. and Miranda planned to head to a friend's house, after which she would return to Gardiner for a 3 p.m. dance rehearsal.

Miranda, like Ashley, loved to dance. At home she would create new moves to Janet Jackson or Pink in the living room. She was excited about an upcoming competition and had been practicing constantly. Miranda also enjoyed the typical other hobbies of a teenager, spending her own money made from baby-sitting on glitter makeup and trendy clothes while hanging out at the mall. She often wore her brown hair pulled back with two long strands framing her attractive face. She dreamed of becoming a model or an actress.

The young girl, however, had her own troubled family history. Jason Gaddis, Miranda's biological father, was still married to Michelle in 1994 when he was indicted on ten felony counts ranging from third-degree rape to custodial interference involving two minor girls. Convicted on six of those counts, Gaddis served nineteen months in prison and was released in September 1996. One of those victims, in a request for a restraining order, claimed Gaddis had threatened to burn her house down and kill her. The restraining order was granted.

Once Jason and Michelle divorced, things would get even worse. Michelle started seeing Brett Edward Mcenaney, who, according to court records, completed tenth-grade special education classes without the ability to read. Mcenaney proceeded to sexually abuse all of Michelle's children, including Miranda. In 1999, the Clackamas County district attorney indicted him on twenty-two counts of sexual abuse in the first degree. Mcenaney was eventually sentenced to more than eighteen years at the Eastern Oregon Correctional Institution.

In her own way, Miranda Gaddis tried to move on. She was outgoing and social, looking to find true friendships and real relationships in spite of all else. She impressed everyone she met with her strong personality. "Resilient" and "determined" were the words friends would later remember her with.

"Love ya," Miranda called out as her mother left the apartment to go to work that March morning at 7:30. Miranda's sisters, eleven-year-old Miriah and fourteen-year-old Marissa, had already left for school.

"Love ya, too," Michelle replied while locking the door behind herself.

After finishing a bowl of cereal, Miranda got ready for school alone, tossing on rhinestone jeans and a hooded sweatshirt. She had to be up the street by 8:15 a.m., where a dozen middle school students who caught the bus from the complex waited. That number had until recently been thirteen.

Miranda missed her friend Ashley, so much so that she had cried on television for her safe return. But in the hushed hallways of Gardiner Middle School, the girls wondered what might have *really* happened to her. The police, so sure that Ashley was a runaway, were not alone in that thinking. Miranda knew that Ashley, like herself, had a troubled past. Ashley's home life, in fact, may have been even worse than Miranda's.

Lori Pond and her daughter, despite the mother's claims, had not been the best of friends. For nearly six months, Ashley had fled the chaos of her own Newell Creek Village apartment to the safety of a neighbor's house, trying to escape the drinking and fighting that were regular occurrences. She moved in with her friend Mallori Weaver, also on the dance team.

Mallori's father, Ward Francis Weaver III, was popular with the kids. Half the neighborhood girls spent time at his house. He was an especially consoling father figure in a sea of neglect and abuse. Weaver, unlike their fathers, showed up at dance meets to cheer the girls on, and had even taken Ashley on a trip to California with other family members. Ward Weaver essentially adopted the troubled girl and treated her like one of his own.

Then, seemingly out of the blue, Ashley had turned on Weaver. She moved back home and even refused to go over to his house again. There were rumors that something sexually inappropriate had happened and possibly a police complaint had been filed. Miranda knew Weaver was hurt by the allegations, learning all about it from Mallori while spending the night at their house for a slumber party on February 23.

Then, as many of the girls speculated, Ashley just up and ran away.

On March 8, Miranda left her home around 8:10 a.m. She locked the door behind herself and slipped her keys into her pocket. The rain was starting to fall harder. Miranda, like Ashley, never made it to the school bus stop that day.

Now two girls would never be seen alive again.

At least by the time Miranda Gaddis disappeared, the Oregon City police were ready to jump into action. After a friend of Miranda's called her mother at work that day to see why she hadn't been in school, Michelle Duffey reported her missing at 4:52 p.m. Four minutes later, two officers were assigned to the case. Within a half hour, another officer showed up at the school. By that evening, authorities were going door-to-door at the Newell Creek Village apartment complex. They even called the FBI in right away.

Police Chief Huiras rightly knew that if a few news crews had shown up for Ashley, filming students at Gardiner Middle School and then hounding him with questions, the media would be all over a *second* disappearance. Danielle van Dam had been abducted in Sabre Springs, California, just the previous month, creating outrage and shock at the unnecessary loss of a child. Now the nation's attention would have a new target — Oregon City.

Huiras wanted to be ready.

The following day, more than thirty officers ignored a steady rain and damp chill to fan out into the nearby woods, calling out Miranda's name as they went. In front of reporters, a bloodhound ran up the steps to the teenager's second-floor apartment before tearing off through the complex.

"They picked up her scent," announced Oregon City police Lieutenant Mike Jarvis. He explained it had led to the local Fred Meyer supermarket across the street, where officers immediately checked a surveillance tape. Added Jarvis, "No definitive information came out of that."

By midday, about fifty FBI agents rolled into Oregon City, setting up a command post on the second floor of the fire department. "Almost every FBI agent in this area who was available was here today," said Beth Ann Steele, the spokeswoman for the FBI's Portland office.

"We're looking at this as an abduction," claimed Charles Mathews, FBI special agent in charge of the case. He felt it was time to take the lead, making the very statement police had avoided with Ashley.

The FBI added that they were now "virtually certain" both teenage girls were kidnapped, and authorities now sought public help in locating them. Agents intended to contact some of the same "persons of interest" who were originally questioned by police when Ashley disappeared. The Gaddis's home computer was being searched in hopes of finding any leads into Miranda's final days and hours. Authorities would look for e-mails and websites she had visited, trying to find out if she had met someone online.

No sooner had authorities made a good showing then police Lt. Mike Jarvis, speaking to reporters, announced, "Truly, right now we've run out of things to do [in the Pond case] and now need to revisit the things we've done." Then, freely stating the obvious, he added, "Frankly, that will happen soon because we have to take a long hard look at similarities and coincidences."

The Oregon City Police Department needed, if not better

investigators, a good PR rep. They were certainly doing nothing to calm the residents of the Newell Creek Village apartment complex. Near panic was setting in.

"If I didn't have a lease, I'd be out of here tomorrow," Jennifer Smith said the Saturday after Miranda disappeared. The mother of three daughters had lived there for four years, but now she wouldn't let her daughter go up one flight of steps alone to play with a friend.

"It's terrifying," Mary Hugill, also a mother, explained. "Most people here can't afford to pack up and move."

Those who could afford it were packing up. "We have a little baby," Hannah Gonzales said while carting toys into a moving van parked in the street.

"My son was crying last night, scared someone was going to come in and take him," said Brandi Williams. "People are very suspicious of it being someone around here . . . someone who knows the neighborhood kids and their schedules."

Some residents felt they had to take matters into their own hands. John Buck was walking around the Newell Creek Village Apartments with a long-barreled pistol in a leather holster under his arm. He had sent his girls to live in Washington with relatives and planned to move to Colorado. "They just fell off the face of the earth," Buck said of the missing girls, who both had played with his daughter.

The following Monday, the Gardiner Middle School bus, instead of picking up kids down the street, drove right up to the front of the complex. The few children waiting were all accompanied by their parents.

Almost predictably, with no crime scene, no witnesses, and seemingly nothing to go on, the investigation led nowhere. Days turned into weeks before, more than four months after Ashley Pond had been deemed a runaway by the Oregon City Police Department, the floodgates of criticism opened.

As experts told the community that they could potentially have a serial killer on their hands, people began to speak up. With two girls gone, Oregon City residents were concerned there might come a third. Questions and outrage began to emerge in various media reports.

"Time was lost there," said John Walsh of *America's Most Wanted*, which featured the case numerous times. "Two days of trying to determine if she [Ashley] is a runaway is two days of lost time. You never assume the child is a runaway."

"When there's a missing child, we go in and assume the worst and hope for the best," said Phil Donegan, the former assistant special agent in charge of the FBI in Oregon. "You have missed opportunities. So the policy is, you go in as if you're facing the worst possible scenario."

Don Martin, Lori Pond's stepfather, said that although Oregon City police had done a "pretty good" job, he wished the department had interviewed Ashley's dance instructor and searched the apartment complex the night she disappeared.

"We felt more should have been done," he said.

Terri Duffey, Miranda's aunt, raised the point that would now begin to haunt the Oregon City Police Department — if only authorities would have used the same resources in Ashley's disappearance as they had in Miranda's, maybe a life could have been saved.

CHAPTER 12

The Gardiner Middle School dance team had been planning a benefit. Miranda Gaddis, her friend Mallori Weaver, and all the other girls wanted to raise money for a reward in Ashley's case. Michelle Rizzo, the dance class teacher, considered canceling the event after March 8. All the girls decided together to go on as planned, but now the March 23 show would contribute toward a reward for both Ashley and Miranda.

On the day of the performance, the Oregon City High School gymnasium was filled to capacity with scores of dancing teenagers, not only from Gardiner Middle School but also from other surrounding schools. Eight hundred teary-eyed parents and children filled the wooden bleachers. In the front row sat Michelle Duffey and Lori Pond, who was now seven months pregnant. Both mothers wore T-shirts with the girls' pictures on them.

"My daughter is missing" was written across the bottom of Michelle's. Other relatives had their own shirts, each changed accordingly with the words "niece" or "granddaughter."

In the back, people bought baked goods, raffle tickets, and

pins with pictures of the missing girls decorated with red hearts. Many stuffed extra dollars into an oversized plastic container for contributions. Portland Trailblazer cheerleaders signed autographs. One stand, selling DNA kits for parents to store samples from their children in case of kidnapping, was seen doing a brisk business. The reward, which had climbed to $60,000 before Saturday's event, would now have thousands more.

Miranda's mother had already done the television circuit, pleading for any information that could lead to her daughter's safe return. Speaking on NBC's *Today* show, Michelle said she believed the girls were familiar with their abductor.

"We are all thinking it is someone they knew, because of the way the girls were, especially Miranda," she said. "It would have been a really big fight if it would have been someone she didn't know."

Lori went on CBS's *Early Show*, but the traveling weighed on her already heavy mind. Trying to keep interest in the case alive, she began meeting with reporters outside her apartment, echoing the same sorrow and suspicion as Michelle. Tired and subdued, her eyes red from crying, she said, "I'm grateful that the whole community is watching. I don't want anybody to ever have to go through this again."

Offers of food, clothing and support were coming to the families. Gift baskets filled with fresh fruit and cookies were left at their front door. Friends and even strangers were asking if they needed anything at all.

Ward Weaver III, Mallori's father, was one member of the community who tried to get the Duffeys' minds off their sorrows. He invited the entire family over to his neighboring house for a barbecue. When the Duffeys declined, he asked Michelle out for drinks. Later, he offered to take Miranda's younger sister, Miriah, to Disneyland with his own daughter, just as he had done with Ashley.

Then Weaver, who was five-foot-eleven and 180 pounds with thinning brown hair and a mustache, started driving by their apartment slowly, dark glasses on his face, and smiling . . .

As the months passed, the Oregon City Police Department and the FBI had more than enough suspects to look at. The list of convicted and violent sex offenders stretched pages long.

On Miranda's side was her father, Jason Gaddis Sr., convicted of rape charges. Michelle's subsequent boyfriend, Brett Mcenaney, had been convicted of not only molesting Miranda but all of Michelle's other children, as well. And then there was Brian Daniel, a friend of Michelle's who hung out all the time at their apartment before murdering an associate in 1998. On Ashley's side was her natural father, Wesley Roettger Jr., who had been charged with forty counts of sexual abuse against Ashley. Lori's father, Steven Alan Davis, was also convicted of molesting his second wife's daughter.

Investigators obviously had their hands full before even venturing beyond the victims' own Newell Creek Village apartments.

More than forty Oregon City cops and FBI agents were now working full-time on a joint task force. They had received more than two thousand tips and interviewed thousands of people. With no evidence and no witnesses, the case stayed cold. The FBI claimed that even behavioral scientists from Quantico, Virginia, were stumped. Roadblocks were set up throughout town and more flyers were passed out to motorists. A billboard was erected with the girls' pictures on it, begging the public for any information.

Kristi Sloan, Ward Weaver's second ex-wife, was one of the people who had driven by those billboards and had followed every detail of the emerging story. Initially, when Ashley disappeared, she was as confused as everyone else in

Oregon City. Then, as soon as Miranda Gaddis went missing, her suspicions grew.

Kristi had divorced Weaver in 2000 and was still all too familiar with what he was up to. She considered his four kids from a previous marriage to Maria Shaw, including Mallori, her own. Maria had distanced herself from Weaver after their divorce, filing a restraining order against him. Kristi, on the other hand, knew that Ashley had moved into her ex-husband's home for a long stretch of 2001. She also knew that Miranda had spent the night at Weaver's house as recently as Saturday, February 23, to celebrate Mallori's birthday.

Now, with two girls missing, it all fell into place, and Kristi immediately called investigators. Only months later would the world be listening to the very details that the police learned in March. On CNN's *Connie Chung Tonight*, Kristi explained what happened.

"Did you ever suspect Ward of being connected to these two kidnappings?" asked the popular television host.

"When Ashley first came up missing, I did not suspect him of having something to do with it," replied Kristi. "A lot of people at the time thought she was just a runaway. When Miranda came up missing . . . I starting putting everything together, thinking that he [Weaver] had something to do with it. There were just too many coincidences on how the girls came up missing. They both went to the same school as his youngest daughter. They were all on the same dance team. And they both came up missing on their way to school."

"Now, both mothers of Miranda and Ashley told me that their daughters would never get into a car of a stranger. Do you believe that Ashley and Miranda might have gotten into the car, if indeed, Ward had driven by?" Chung asked.

"Yes, I do strongly believe what their mothers said, that neither of those girls would have gotten into a car with somebody that they did not know. But Ward Weaver is not a man that was a stranger to them. And I believe that if he offered them a ride, that one of the girls would have taken it from him, just because he was somebody that they both knew."

"Did you ever go to the police because of your suspicions that your ex-husband may have been involved in these kidnappings?"

"I went to the FBI. The FBI had interviewed several people, including myself, further family members of Ward . . . I told them that I was the ex-wife of Ward Weaver and that I did not know for sure if he had any involvement in the disappearances of the two girls from Oregon City, but just to make me feel better and for me to be able to rest and my conscience, that, you know, I would like to talk with them."

"But why would you suspect him of actually kidnapping the girls?" Chung queried.

"He is a really aggressive person, and when things don't go right his way, he has to find another way to take them out," Kristi responded.

"Has Ward Weaver ever been violent to you or to your kids?"

"We don't have any kids together, but I was raising the four of his kids, which I call my kids. I still see them all of the time. We did have an incident back in 1995 where there was a police report filed with a restraining order, where I was taken to the hospital. I was violently attacked in the middle of the night by him with a cast-iron frying pan and hit over the head several times. And he told me that his intention was to kill me."

"My gosh!" exclaimed Chung, her eyes going wide. Kristi hadn't even found time to explain, as she would in future interviews, how Weaver told her she "was lucky." He had considered using a butcher's knife.

"After you went to the police, was Ward questioned by

them?" Chung asked. "As I understand it, he was even given a lie-detector test, and according to some reports, he did not pass the lie-detector test."

"Not only according to some reports, words out of his own mouth, he failed the lie-detector test."

"Did you ever ask him if he did, indeed, kidnap those two girls?"

"I never came out directly and asked him," Kristi answered. "But three days after Miranda came up missing, which is the second girl, he had a hole dug in his backyard and cemented it to pour for a hot tub. And they dug and cemented in the middle of the winter and in the rain."

Kristi Sloan wasn't the only one who was suspicious enough of Ward Weaver III to talk to authorities. Harry Oakes was a dog handler with the International K9 Search and Rescue organization who volunteered to help look for Ashley. Lori Pond had responded to a letter he wrote offering to help, and he showed up at her Newell Creek apartment to obtain a belonging with Ashley's scent on March 7, the day before Miranda disappeared. His dog, Valerie, then went to work, searching the canyon below the apartment complex.

According to Oakes, his dog gave him a "death alert" in the canyon, directly downhill from Weaver's property. Oakes explained that Valerie may have picked up scents as a result of rain seeping downhill from there. A "death alert" means the search dog detects the presence or former presence of a human body.

On March 15, now with two girls missing, Oakes and Valerie showed up at Weaver's home on South Beavercreek Road. Oakes had identified himself as a private search-dog handler to Weaver's son Alex and obtained Ward Weaver's permission, by telephone, to search the property.

According to the *Portland Tribune*, Weaver told Oakes to

go ahead with his search with one caveat: "He did ask for me to 'stay away from the freshly poured concrete' as he just got it laid out on the ground and didn't want it 'messed up,' " Oakes said. Weaver went on to tell him he intended to install a hot tub on the spot.

Slowly, Oakes and Valerie made their way around the property, inching ever closer to the freshly poured concrete slab. Then, once again, Valerie gave a death alert. The spot she was moving frantically toward was precisely where the fresh cement was drying.

Oakes submitted his findings to the authorities, emphasizing his results. But as far as the police were concerned, Oakes was not a credible source. Apparently, he and Valerie had a long, negative history with other search-dog handlers. One of those handlers was interviewed by the *Portland Tribune* and said, Valerie "wouldn't alert in a graveyard."

Just as Kristi Sloan had done, Oakes would later tell a national television audience about the findings he gave the police in March. He was interviewed on a FOX news show by host Rita Cosby.

"Your dog, Valerie, picked up an unusual scent back in March. Tell us about that," Cosby began.

"Well, we obtained permission from Lori Pond to come in privately and do a private search for Ashley," Oakes explained. "We obtained the scent article of Ashley, gave it to search dog Valerie, and she tracked Ashley's scent to the back of Ward's house. I then contacted Ward by telephone and asked permission to conduct a search of his property. He said yes, just stay away from the back cement area that he had just poured . . . My dog alerted in the cement area, as well as at a shed behind the house."

"This was back in March, though, you're telling me, that . . ."

"That's correct."

"They actually picked up the scent? What happened [with the police]?"

"You'll have to ask them that."

Authorities had searched the property themselves after Weaver agreed to their request. Their dogs, unlike Valerie, had indicated there was nothing suspicious on the property.

CHAPTER 13

Jim Redden is an experienced crime reporter who had been following the Ashley Pond and Miranda Gaddis story for the *Portland Tribune* from the day the first girl went missing. Redden loves writing about crime because, as he claims, "it shows how people really live." And when he covers a case, "I always set out to solve it."

Fresh out of the University of Oregon in the early '80s, Redden soon grew bored with an assignment to cover a man who had already been arrested. The reporter decided to make a difference, going after a local cocaine dealer for his first paper, the *Willamette Week*. Diving into the seedy underworld of club life, he talked to the friends and associates of his suspect. Entitled "Portland Vice," the article eventually helped take a hardened criminal off the streets.

Later Redden took it up a notch, going after a murderer. The Starry Night was the biggest club in Portland at the time, run by a lowlife named Larry Hurwitz. After a publicity director mysteriously disappeared, for years Redden doggedly pursued any and all leads. Despite the fact that a body was never found and investigators failed to file charges, Redden was sure that Hurwitz had killed his former associate when the man threatened to expose a financial crisis at the club.

Forty articles and a massive lawsuit later, the reporter pushed authorities to go after Hurwitz for tax evasion charges. Once the suspect was safely behind bars, others came forward to implicate the club owner in the original murder. Some twenty years after Redden wrote his first piece on Hurwitz, the man was convicted for murder, and the lawsuit thrown out of court.

By July 2002, with the authorities in Oregon City saying they were no closer to finding a culprit in their current case, Redden received an interesting phone call.

A friend of the Ponds informed the reporter that members of the family were suspicious of Weaver, and Redden heard two details that had him reaching for his notepad. The first was that Ashley had lived at Weaver's home for a period of time. The second was that Weaver had poured a concrete slab in his backyard shortly after Miranda disappeared in March. The reporter had no idea how much more authorities knew or even that Weaver was, in fact, the FBI's prime suspect. But where the police and FBI had yet to execute a search warrant, Redden smelled a killer.

With a little work, Redden learned a few other things, also details that had to have already been discovered by investigators. By checking Weaver's Oregon criminal record, he found the prior arrest for assault on his now ex-wife Kristi Sloan. The case was eventually dismissed when Kristi failed to show up for a hearing. Both Kristi and his previous wife, Maria Shaw, had taken out restraining orders against Weaver, who was arrested again for violating those orders.

On the trail of a hot story, the reporter approached the front of Weaver's rundown home on South Beavercreek Road the following Sunday, hoping to catch him by surprise. Ward Weaver answered the door wearing a dirty white tank top and cutoff jeans. After Redden identified himself, he asked if Weaver would talk to him about the missing girls. After hesitating for a moment, then looking the reporter up and down, Weaver invited him in. Redden noticed an expensive home entertainment center nearly filling one living room wall, and two paintings of unicorns hanging in the hall near the kitchen.

Although Weaver seemed nervous, many interview subjects were, especially when surprised early in the morning. As Redden took notes, Weaver explained how both missing girls were friends with his daughter, Mallori. When Redden asked how well he knew them, Weaver immediately volunteered that Ashley had lived at his house for five months the previous summer after Lori Pond "dumped her off on the way to a party." He said Miranda had visited only a few times.

Weaver then freely admitted to Redden he was the FBI's "prime suspect." After Redden asked why, Weaver explained that Ashley had accused him of molesting her. According to Weaver, Ashley made the accusation after they had a petty argument. Weaver denied any wrongdoing, saying the police had looked into the allegations and never charged him. But, Weaver said, Lori Pond, still bitter, told the FBI about the accusations.

As Redden sat there in Weaver's living room, one question came to mind. Looking Weaver in the eye, he asked, "Did you do it?"

Although Weaver seemed temporarily stunned by the question, he adamantly denied having anything to do with their disappearances.

"Ashley was a part of this family," he replied.

By August, with the hot summer wearing on, other pieces began coming together for Redden. Only one face grew clear on that complex puzzle — Ward Weaver III's.

When Ashley had lived at the Weavers', according to numerous sources, the two developed a strangely intimate relationship, almost as if they were an item. A paternal aunt of Ashley Pond's, Elaine Garfield, said that no member of Ashley's immediate family could talk to the girl without going through Weaver first. In addition to that, Weaver's girlfriend during that time period, Tammy Place, hadcomplained that the twelve-year-old was getting more attention than she. Tammy even had to sleep elsewhere in the house to make room for Ashley in Weaver's bed.

Then Ashley had admitted to her mother's boyfriend, James Keightley, that Weaver had molested her. Ashley initially didn't want to tell anyone else. She was still suffering the fallout from the earlier allegations against her father, Wesley Roettger Jr. Ashley had said several months after her father's arrest in December 2000 that she wished she had not told authorities about what had happened and didn't want to testify against him. Because her dad was in jail, her half siblings had been taken into protective custody, and she could no longer visit them. Even so, Keightley insisted Ashley go to her mother, which she did.

The Pond family then supposedly submitted a complaint against Weaver in August 2001. A spokesman for the Clackamas County District Attorney's office told the *Portland Tribune* that those allegations were reported to the state child protective services agency as soon as they learned of them. But what happened to those allegations after that is unclear. There is no public record showing that allegations against Weaver were referred to Oregon City police, which would have had jurisdiction to investigate Weaver based on his residence in Oregon City.

One of Ashley Pond's elementary schoolteachers had also filed a report regarding the same incident. Linda Virden, who taught at Gaffney Lane Elementary School, said she alerted state authorities after Ashley confided to her that she was molested by Ward Weaver, dating back to September 2001. Virden claimed that Ashley told her, "Linda, Ward didn't rape me, he tried to rape me, I know the difference." Virden then wrongly assumed that the matter was being checked out. Once again, that report fell through the cracks.

In addition to that, Deputy District Attorney Chris Owen also learned of the alleged abuse against Ashley by Weaver. He was prosecuting Ashley's father, Wesley Roettger, in that case when the other allegations came up. As required by law, Owen called the state hot line on August 31, 2001. The child welfare office received Owen's report and instead of faxing it to Oregon City police, passed it along to the Clackamas County Sheriff's office several weeks later. The sheriff's office said it never got the report.

After the twelve-year-old disappeared in early January, Virden, now one of three people who reported Ashley's claims against Weaver, called the Oregon City police to follow up. They had no knowledge of the report. She called four times and even gave them the information again but was never contacted during the investigation into the girls' disappearances.

Jim Redden now knew that the very man who had admitted to him to being the FBI's "prime suspect" would have had a motive to make Ashley disappear. Even if those claims hadn't been lost, with no girl to testify against him, the case would be dead in the water.

And concerning the clue that sparked Redden's initial gut feel — the very thing that originally had him reaching for a notepad and driving to Weaver's home — that concrete slab? It didn't take long to check out Weaver's family background and to learn that more than twenty years earlier his father, Ward F. Weaver Jr., had murdered two people and then buried one in his backyard under a concrete slab.

There were more red flags than on a dynamite storage warehouse, but Ward Weaver III was still a free man.

CHAPTER 14

O n Tuesday, August 13, 2002, a young woman, naked and wrapped only in a blue plastic tarp, desperately waved down a passing motorist on South Beavercreek Road. The nineteen-year-old girlfriend of Francis Weaver, one of Ward Weaver III's three sons, was taken to a nearby shoe store, where she phoned 911. Badly beaten and terrified, she told police that Weaver had raped and threatened to kill her. The victim was taken to Willamette Falls Hospital for evaluation and treatment.

When Francis heard about what his father had allegedly done to his girlfriend, he placed his own 911 call to authorities that evening. In tears, he told a Clackamas County dispatcher that his father told him he had killed Ashley Pond and Miranda Gaddis and that he was moving to Mexico. The chilling admission was reported by *The Oregonian*, quoting a dispatch summary.

Police stopped Weaver as he drove on I-205. He was arrested and booked into the Clackamas County Jail, and his bail was set at $1,000,000. Police then searched Weaver's house on August 14, finding that he had moved most of his belongings out, lending credence to Francis's claim that his father may have been preparing to move. Still, apparently no evidence was found, and authorities left.

Despite Francis Weaver's assertion that his father had killed Ashley and Miranda, Police Chief Huiras, talking about how the investigation into the rape might afford clues into the unsolved abductions, said, "We haven't developed anything from this investigation that ties into that case."

For nearly two weeks Weaver's property was left unsecured, during which time various people came and went. On August 15, Weaver's friend Roger Stevens went into the shed to retrieve his own possessions stored there. Stevens told the *Tribune* that the shed contained black plastic lawn bags full of things that did not belong to him, so he left them there. Then, on August 16, numerous media representatives were on the property, filming and taking photographs.

The property owner, Steve Hopkins, from whom Weaver had rented the house, arrived the next morning. Hopkins told the *Tribune* that he noticed nothing unusual about the shed except for five or six fly strips "totally covered with flies."

One local resident, who along with everyone else in town had now learned of Ward Weaver III's father's murderous history, walked straight onto the property and stuck a "Dig Me Up!" sign on the new concrete slab in the backyard.

Finally, on Saturday, August 24, investigators returned to Weaver's home on South Beavercreek Road. They still hadn't secured a new warrant regarding the murder charges, but Weaver had consented to an additional search with the hope to "bring closure to the families," according to his lawyer, Timothy Lyons. Investigators would know soon enough what exactly Weaver and his attorney meant by that statement.

Tragically, inside the shed in the backyard, they found the body of Miranda Gaddis, heartlessly stuffed into a cardboard box. The following day, investigators returned to the scene with a backhoe to dig up the concrete slab poured in March. Underneath, stuffed into a barrel, they found Ashley Pond.

FBI spokeswoman Beth Anne Steele commented to the media that possibly the bodies were not there when their dogs searched the area months earlier. Oregon City police, on the other hand, at least acknowledged that Ashley's body had "probably" been there since mid-March, when the concrete slab was poured. They also added that Ward Weaver was now their prime suspect in the case, joining the FBI with that brilliant deduction.

After police erected a fence around the property, it soon became a makeshift memorial. For months, the public had hoped and prayed with the families for a safe return of the girls. Two middle school students, yet to even experience the joys of life, were robbed of everything. The emotional outpouring was tremendous.

Thousands of bouquets of flowers, cards, and stuffed animals were left on the sidewalk and tucked between the metal links. One note read, "Two girls we never knew, but touched our lives forever — they'll live forever in our hearts. Wherever you are, keep dancing." Another read, "We'll always remember our angels of Oregon City." Rikki Depue, a fourteen-year-old friend of both girls, tucked yet another message in the wire: "You are still alive to me."

On Thursday, August 29, mourners gathered at the high school for a service. Oregon City Christian Church youth pastor Ken Swatman opened the memorial by asking those in attendance to remember "two beautiful young ladies who endured so much in their lives." Screens had been set up on the roof of the school to broadcast the service live to people on a softball field.

"I like to do gymnastics. I can do the rings and the bars, and I'm practicing on the beam," Meladee Beeson, Ashley's

English teacher, read from the girl's journal. A video collage showed snapshots from family albums — Miranda sitting on Santa Claus's lap as a young girl, Ashley playing video games in a sleeping bag. Quotes from friends with their fondest memories ran with the photos.

A funeral for Ashley was held on Saturday, August 31. A service for Miranda was held at 1 p.m. on Tuesday, September 3. Both were for family and friends only. They all needed a break from the cameras to cry in peace.

Steve Hopkins, the owner of the rental property, announced that Weaver's former home would be demolished. "When [police] gave the place back to me yesterday, I decided this place is going away in a hurry. I'm going to demolish the building and let it breathe and heal so people can get back to normal."

A few days later, crews using heavy equipment tore into the single-story house. The FBI and the Oregon City Police Department agreed to the decision, saying they had collected all the evidence they needed from the house.

As sorrow was replaced by anger in Oregon City over what had happened to Ashley Pond and Miranda Gaddis, the magnitude of the tragedy set in. There was no simple answer, only more questions. There had been failures at every level.

"Detectives and police stood out here all hours with posters and they were right here all along," said Terri Duffey, Miranda's aunt. Over the last few months reporters had prodded the families of both victims to criticize the police and FBI, which they refrained from doing. Now it was just too painful. "They came in and out of that driveway a hundred times and they were right there, I mean *right there*, and we couldn't do anything."

But the blame did not end there. An especially poignant editorial, written by David Reinhard, an associate editor, appeared in the *Oregonian* in early September, describing the "untold" tragedy that had occurred.

"Something needs to be said, and said publicly, about all that helped savage the lives of Ashley and Miranda long before they died . . . Call them poor choices, mistakes or sins. Call them what you will. But what we see in the Oregon City story is a long string of unwise or unwholesome actions that compromised the lives of these two girls. It's a stark lesson — several lessons, really — in what happens when parents' choices and living arrangements put children at risk."

Reinhard, fully aware that "no one wants the mothers, who have suffered life's ultimate pain, to be hurt further," still felt impelled to raise the issue. The family history couldn't be ignored. He included the fathers' "hideous crimes against [their own] children."

And then, speaking on the *Today* show to Soledad O'Brien, Ashley's sixth-grade teacher, Linda Virden, described yet another failure.

Virden said, "The case worker I was talking to said that she would take all of this information down and be sure to get it to Ashley's case worker and that it would be taken care of. I thought that, at that point, it was pretty clear that they would act on it and that if I could in any way help, that they would be in touch with me. But I never heard back from them."

When Virden had called to follow up after Ashley disappeared, "There was just this silence on the other end of the phone and then this police officer said, 'I have the complete file in front of me from Ashley's case worker, and there is no record of you ever filing a report.'"

Two months later, when Ashley's friend Miranda Gaddis disappeared, Virden had again called police to remind them that Weaver's daughter, Mallori, had been a friend of both missing girls.

"Nobody listened to me. And nobody seemed to care . . .

It wasn't enough. And we lost both of them."

But in the end, although all those things failed to help Miranda Gaddis or Ashley Pond and could have potentially saved their lives, only one thing ultimately killed these girls — Ward Weaver III.

CHAPTER 15

Although many details of Ward Weaver III's past were being exposed as he was arrested in August 2002, few people understood that the roots of his violent urges could have held up a Douglas fir in the Oregon forest.

From the day Ward III came into the world on April 6, 1963, the firstborn child to his parents, Ward Weaver Jr. and Patricia, the boy very well may have been on a collision course with hell. Much of what is known about the Weaver family's history came to light when Ward Jr. (Ward III's father), a long-distance truck driver, was tried in California's Kern County Superior Court in 1984 for the kidnap, rape, and murder of twenty-three-year-old Barbara Levoy and the murder of her boyfriend, eighteen-year-old Robert Radford.

Ward Jr. had picked the couple up along the roadside after their car broke down in Tehachapi, California, on February 5, 1981. At some point he pulled his truck over and asked Robert for help adjusting the load in his cab. Leaving Levoy in the front seat, both men went to the back, where Ward Jr. bludgeoned Radford on the head with a metal pipe. He left him on the roadside after crushing his skull to a pulp.

For the next few hours, Ward Jr. repeatedly raped and sodomized Levoy, until, in a violent struggle to free herself, she bit his thumb and he strangled her to death with a ragged baby diaper. Then, in a bizarre precursor of events that would unfold in his son's life twenty-one years later, the father stashed Levoy's body under a concrete slab in his backyard, proudly telling his wife that the platform would help keep her feet dry when she hung out the laundry.

Ward Jr. was already serving a sentence for rape and conspiracy to commit murder before he was charged with the Levoy-Radford murders. As if those misdeeds weren't bad enough, there were others. The crime that originally earned him a forty-two year sentence occurred in May 1981, when Ward Jr. picked up two teenage hitchhikers, David Galbraith and Michelle D. (her name was withheld from court records). Ward Jr. then arranged for a friend to shoot the eighteen-year-old boy while he repeatedly raped the fifteen-year-old girl. Galbraith miraculously survived the shooting and gave cops a perfectly detailed description of his assailant's truck.

Stuck in prison, Ward Jr. was unable to contain his pride at the double murder he *had* gotten away with in February, so he bragged to his cellmate at San Quentin, Ricky Gibson, who quickly ratted him out. Authorities dug up the cement slab in Ward Jr.'s backyard, under which Barbara Levoy was found.

By the time Ward Jr. was tried for the Levoy-Radford murders, he was long since divorced from his wife, Patricia. Even so, she showed up to testify in court, explaining why he may have gone berserk and strangled Levoy when she bit his thumb.

"He hates being bitten," Patricia said, testifying that she once bit his hand when they were "wrestling" in the car, and he became furious and began choking her. On another occasion, Patricia went on, she bit his hand and he grabbed her by the neck, looking dazed and glassy-eyed.

Ward Jr. later told Patricia he didn't know why he'd choked her, but he relayed a story about his mother, Dorothy, biting him so hard as a child that she drew blood. Patricia claimed an unrepentant Dorothy confirmed the story and even recommended biting as a child-rearing tool.

There were other signs the family matriarch, Dorothy, was not exactly a doting mom. She had routinely doled out whippings to her children, Ward Jr. and his sister, Katie. Another witness testified that Dorothy was a "man-hater," who once hoisted a butcher knife and screamed she'd like to "cut off all their penises," Kern County prosecutor Ron Shumaker told *The Oregonian* newspaper.

Ward Jr. and Patricia had married in 1962, and then moved in with the coldhearted Dorothy and her husband, the original Ward Francis Weaver. Some vicious fights marked the new marriage. In talking with a court-appointed psychiatrist after a previous 1977 conviction for clubbing a woman named Bonnie Brown on the head with a baseball bat, Ward Jr. recounted that in the early years of his marriage to Patricia, he "assaulted his wife several times and volunteered for the army so that he would be killed," court records say.

So whether to flee his own guilt over abusing Patricia or just to get away from a marriage that wasn't working, Ward Jr. signed up for the U.S. Army and went to Vietnam at the height of the fighting, starting a two-year stint in 1968. Patricia was left behind with three small kids. Ward III was just five when his father headed off to war on a distant continent.

In Vietnam, Ward Jr. would see some heavy combat, and in the opinion of several court-appointed psychiatrists who examined him years later, he appeared to have symptoms associated with post-traumatic stress disorder.

One psychiatrist, Dr. Clyde Donahoe, said Ward Jr. told

him he had either witnessed or participated in "the killing of women and children, mutilation of dead bodies, mutilation of live people, inadvertent air strikes or ambushes on our own or friendly troops, use of white phosphorus or napalm, torture of prisoners, mercy killing, watching a buddy die in a gruesome manner, taking human body parts as trophies, bagging dead bodies, deliberate killing of old women, men, or children, and the routine killing of prisoners."

The Levoy-Radford trial, already grim and somber due to the gruesome deaths the victims suffered, edged further into the depths of human hell as testimony about Ward Jr.'s cold, dark psyche flowed from the mouths of witnesses like his sister, Katie.

Katie testified that her older brother began to terrorize her at a young age. When she was six, he chopped off one of her fingers while playing with a hatchet. A year later, he tied her to a tree and threatened to hang her. She didn't believe him until he began to place a noose around her neck, when she started to scream hysterically. Ward Jr. didn't hang her, but left her tied to the tree for hours.

There were more horrific incidents. Once when Katie was in a field near their rural home, Ward Jr. stampeded a herd of cattle into the area, and later told her he'd done it on purpose. He also locked her in a toolshed and set it on fire. He finally let her out when she screamed and pounded on the door, but the flames grew out of control and started a forest fire. Heavy-handed Dorothy punished both children for the fiasco.

When Katie was nine, her brother tied her up and inserted sticks into her vagina. When she was twelve, he raped her and told her she was pregnant to torment her. Around that time, she witnessed her brother and a pal torture a cat, rubbing sandpaper on its rear end and then dousing it with turpentine. Katie managed to get her friends to beat Ward Jr.

up in retaliation for his cruelty. But when her parents found out, they gave her a whipping, according to court records.

And if that testimony was gut-wrenching, other testimony was simply bizarre.

Del Roy Barnett, a friend and co-worker of Ward Jr., said that after his buddy returned from Vietnam, he sometimes "talked to himself or unseen people."

Ward Jr. himself would tell psychiatrists that he heard voices in his head, one from an evil male with no name who urged him to do bad things, and the other, a female voice named "Ladell," who urged him to do good. Ladell, coincidentally, was the name of one of his high school girlfriends, according to his sister's testimony. The panel of psychiatrists who examined Ward were split on the issue of whether he really heard voices or was simply faking to bolster his insanity defense.

But several psychiatrists, including Dr. Alfred Owre Jr., reported that Ward Jr. suffered from "distorted relationships" with women, perhaps a legacy of Dorothy's man-hating ways and harsh childhood punishments. Owre reported finding "sadomasochistic features. The defendant derives pleasure from suffering at women's hands, but when stressed, he derives an emotional relief from inflicting pain upon them."

Dr. John Wilson opined that Ward Jr. was a "paranoid schizophrenic," a condition that began developing very early in childhood "as a result of sexual and physical abuse by both his parents, especially his mother," according to court documents. Other doctors also mentioned child abuse as a factor in Ward Jr.'s mental illness, but specifics are not detailed in court papers.

Ironically, despite all Dorothy did to hurt him, Ward Jr. would proudly tell psychiatrists he believed he had "telepathic communication with his mother."

With or without a psychic bond, Ward Jr. remained tied to his mother's apron strings, even as a grown man. "He did nothing without Mama," Kern County prosecutor Ron Shumaker told *The Oregonian*.

Ward Jr. even called his mother to get her blessing before he confessed to the Levoy-Radford murders in August 1982. After Dorothy visited her son and told him "to tell the truth," Ward Jr. gave cops a full account of the grisly crime, down to the last detail of how he handled Levoy's body.

First, he dug a hole and buried Levoy in a secluded spot outside his hometown of Oroville, where he had killed her. He drove into town to see his wife, who was working late at a local restaurant. Then he drove back to the scene, dug up the body, and brought it home in the trunk of his wife's car. With his three kids in the house, Ward Jr. dug a shallow grave on his property and buried the body again. He had already been digging trenches in the yard for a sewer line, so he told his ten-year-old son, Rodney, and another boy to keep digging while he went on the road in his truck to deliver a load. Some weeks later, when he returned, he exhumed the body yet again, and this time moved it to a deeper grave in the backyard, which he sealed with concrete and built a wooden platform atop.

Upon hearing of the discovery of Ashley and Miranda's bodies on Ward III's property — Ashley buried under a concrete slab, and Miranda stashed in a box in the shed — prosecutor Ron Shumaker, who helped put Ward Jr. on death row for the Levoy-Radford murders, wondered about the eerie similarities between the father's and the son's crimes.

Ward Jr. had made the unwitting Rodney help dig the trench in which he stashed Levoy's body before covering the spot with concrete. Was it more than coincidence that Ward III had used his son Alexander, age seventeen, to help him dig and bury barrels underground, one of which, unbeknownst to his son, contained Ashley's remains? Had Ward III used his father's trial as a blueprint for his later crimes? Was he trying to fill his shoes?

"You see something like this, almost a copycat thing, and you wonder," said Shumaker.

CHAPTER 16

The marriage of Ward Jr. and Patricia ended either while he was still in Vietnam or very shortly after he returned. By 1971, Ward Jr. had a second wife, Barbara, and had started on a new batch of kids, including son Rodney, who was born that year. Patricia also remarried and took Ward III and his two sisters into a new home. There was apparently little or no contact between the first Weaver kids and their father and his new family.

Rodney Weaver recently told *The Oregonian* that his father one day casually mentioned the kids from his first marriage. Ward Jr. kept a faded picture of young Ward III and his two sisters hanging on the living room wall of his Oroville, California, home, but they did not visit.

"I wondered about them sometimes," Rodney recalled plaintively. He didn't meet his half brother until 1995, and by that time, he was twenty-four and Ward III was thirty-two.

Tammi, Ward III's youngest sister, said life after their mom divorced Ward Jr. and remarried went from bad to worse. In an off-camera interview with KGW-TV in Portland, Tammi said her stepfather, whom she did not name, often severely beat all the children in her family, including Ward III. In turn, an increasingly angry young Ward III began striking out at Tammi with frequent physical attacks and BB-gun shootings.

Soon, Ward III would escalate from slaps, punches, and air-rifle attacks to much worse. In 1981, when he was eighteen, another unnamed female relative alleged he had beaten and raped her repeatedly over the previous five- or six-year period, beginning when she was about eight or nine and ending when she was fourteen. The relative, now in her thirties, told *The Oregonian* the abuse, both sexual and physical, occurred a "couple times a week," but she did not tell anyone because he threatened to kill her.

Recalling the early phase of her abuse by Ward III, the relative said, "There was a couple times he held me back while he let the neighbor kid beat me up, and I remember — I was about eight — him and the kid walking away with Ward's arm around his shoulder, just laughing, and I am sitting on the steps crying and all beat up."

Finally, when the victim was fourteen, another family member witnessed a sexual attack by Ward III and told the girl's mother. The abuse was reported to Portland, Oregon, police and Multnomah County juvenile authorities. They declined to prosecute because Ward III was about to enlist in the U.S. Navy, and investigators expressed doubts about the victim's "stability and reliability."

But a close childhood friend of the victim, June Theeler of Portland, said she was told about the alleged abuse at the time it was taking place. Theeler recalled the girl coming to her house "bruised and with a bloody nose." Theeler said she not only believes her friend told the truth about Ward III's abuses but said she herself fought off an attack by him when she was sixteen, after he returned home from a stint in the military.

"He tried to take my underwear off me," Theeler told *The Oregonian*. "It scared me to death. I started kicking him and screaming."

By this time, Ward III had a girlfriend, Maria Shaw. According to Theeler, Maria was sleeping on the first floor of the house when Ward tried to rape Theeler upstairs. Theeler said she did not report the incident because she feared her parents would find out.

"That was my mistake," she acknowledged.

Ward III, just like his father, would only grow more vicious.

In 1984, there was important family business to attend to in Bakersfield, California. Ward III's father — the same man who had left him at age five to volunteer for Vietnam, and then dropped out of his life and relegated him to a photo on the wall in his home with his second wife, Barbara — was about to go on trial for the Levoy-Radford murders.

And for some reason, Ward III just had to be there.

Prosecutor Ron Shumaker recalled Ward III, who was barely twenty, showing up at the Bakersfield courthouse in 1984 and then complaining to Kern County sheriff's deputies that "locals were harassing him because he shared his father's name."

On August 4 of that year, with his dad's double-murder trial in full swing, Ward III took time out to marry Maria, right there in Bakersfield. At least some courthouse observers had to be whispering, "Who in their right mind would marry into the Weaver family?"

In any case, after his dad's trial and his own honeymoon ended, Ward III and his first wife would have four children: Francis, Alexander, Mark, and Mallori. Then, in a May 21, 1993, application for a restraining order, Maria accused Weaver of abusing those four kids and of beating and threatening to kill her.

"He abuse [sic] the children," she wrote. "He said he will

have me shot and he hit my kids and he give me black eye and he had broken my coffee table, broke the door, broke my lamps and a lot more other things, children are afraid of their dad."

When asked to put her phone number on the document, she wrote: "NO PHONE CAN'T AFFORD YET, spouse stealing money all the time I have my check."

Maria and Ward's divorce became final on March 9,1995. She initially had custody of the kids, but when her "domestic associate" Daniel Shaw, whom she later married, "beat the children w/belt resulting in injury," the kids were released to their father on April 21, 1997, court records show.

In the ensuing years, some of the kids returned to their mother Maria Shaw's home, but Mallori remained with Ward III until the day of his arrest for raping Francis's girlfriend. She is reportedly in the care of a relative at this time.

In a recent interview, Alexander Weaver described his father's crimes as "crazy and disappointing . . . Other than my sister [Mallori], I think it hit me second hardest because I loved my dad," he told Matt Lauer of NBC's *Today Show*.

Ward III's oldest son, Francis, speaking with CNN's Connie Chung, said he grew up seeing his mother and brothers abused by his dad. "People as a society look up to their fathers. I remember growing up always trying to make my dad look better than he was. He really wasn't that great of a father at all, or ever."

A recently unsealed confidential court document provides even more evidence of Ward III's demented mind. In 1986, he had been convicted of bashing a sixteen-year-old female family friend with a concrete block. He admitted to a probation officer he had a violent temper and once he "blows," anyone around him "is likely to get it, and that's just too bad for them," reported *The Oregonian*.

Ward III attacked the sixteen-year-old girl, who was with

her fifteen-year-old sister, on June 16, 1986, after he called them to ask for a ride home from a local bowling alley. Ward III, the probation report said, had been drinking heavily and had also smoked marijuana and consumed a gram of methamphetamine, a deadly form of chemical speed.

The girls said Ward III was "swearing" about his wife, Maria, and didn't even seem to know who they were when he attacked them in a parking lot, where they had stopped so he could urinate on the ride home. The girls ran to a local bus station and called police.

The following day, Ward III attacked another unidentified female acquaintance in her home. The woman was awakened when he placed his hand over her mouth, squeezed her throat, and ordered her to keep quiet. She kicked free and ran for help, *The Oregonian* reported.

"He loses control," wrote Judith Buell, a deputy probation officer in Solano County, "and claims he cannot stop himself until it runs its course. The defendant admits a building rage and a desire to harm his victims to effect release for his negative feelings.

"He denies any sexual intent and is unable to state how he would have proceeded if not thwarted by his victims."

Ward III admitted the attacks were unprovoked, the report said. In a handwritten statement included in that report, he asked the court to send him to prison, saying incarceration would "do me good."

When reports of Ward Jr.'s murderous past came to light after his son was fingered as the killer of Ashley and Miranda, the nation was left to wonder what role a father plays in shaping a son.

From his cell on death row, Ward Jr. himself was pondering similar questions in an essay he posted on Humanwrites.com, a website devoted to philosophical musings:

Who's to Blame??

A baby is born and the first toy the father gets him to play with is a toy gun and when the child gets old enough to walk, he goes around pointing the gun at his parents and others saying, "Bang, bang, you're dead!" And the parents exclaim, "Oh, how cute."

The father teaches him to shoot real guns and if he shoots well, his father doesn't praise him like the boy is looking for in a father, but rather puts more pressure on the boy by the father telling everyone his son shoots as is expected of the offspring of his family, but will also improve . . . Then he goes to war or whatever you want to call it and kills, kills, kills, and . . . it makes him sick to be reminded by the medals and people around him of what he has been made to grow up into at this point.

Later something happens and he kills someone and the same people that put medals on him now want to kill him. Who's to blame?

Ward Weaver Jr., California

Free to Kill

CHAPTER 17

Samantha Bree Runnion, a vivacious and bubbly five-year-old, had dark wavy curls that fell below tiny shoulders, brown eyes, and a bright smile that could light up a room. Samantha, or "Mantha," as her family called her, stood only three and a half feet tall and weighed a scant forty pounds. Still, one look at a photograph, one frame of a video clip, was enough to warm the hearts of strangers.

For a nation already on edge, this innocent face would strike a chord like no other when the little girl became the latest addition to a growing list of abducted children.

Samantha was born on July 24, 1996, the only child of Erin Runnion. Erin lovingly called her daughter "Bean" and "Mi Tigrita," or my little tiger. The first nickname highlighted the girl's slight appearance, the second a playful ferocity that was apparent from the very first days of her all-too-short life.

"She looked me right in the eye," Erin recalled of her daughter's birth for NBC's *Dateline*, "and I knew instantly . . . she was stronger than I would ever be."

Erin had met Samantha's father, Derek Jackson, while attending Hampshire College in Amherst, Massachusetts, but the lovers went their separate ways when the little girl was only ten months old. Erin headed back to California, where she had been raised, and began working for British Petroleum, overseeing the accounting of jet fuel allocations at West Coast airports. As a single mom, she had to manage two full-time jobs — raising her daughter and putting food on the table.

The hardworking Erin soon fell for another single parent, Ken Donnelly, a compliance director at an investment firm with a master's degree in business administration. Donnelly had two young kids, Paige, age ten, and Conner, five, by a previous marriage. Samantha loved her new siblings, and everyone moved in together, along with Erin's mom, Virginia.

Concerned with the safety of their Garden Grove neighborhood, in 2000 the extended family relocated to Stanton, California, a city of about 38,000 people located twenty-five miles southeast of Los Angeles. The working-class community had one of the lowest crime rates in the area. Their new home was a small three-bedroom town house in the Smoketree Condominiums, a place where kids freely roamed outdoors, and Erin could rest easier.

As Samantha grew, she did all the things that little girls are supposed to do. She played with a collection of toy horses and dolls, learned to ride a bicycle by the time she was four, and always wore a lavender helmet for safety. She spent hours in the community pool with her friends and would run around with her family's dog, Sierra. The little girl loved animals, or "anything furry," as her mom recalled.

Even though Samantha was technically too young, she

left her preschool playmates behind and learned her numbers and ABCs with the big kids. She was about to start first grade at Ernest O. Lawrence Elementary School, where her favorite subject was reading, in which she excelled.

"An overachiever" was how Donnelly described her.

"She wasn't of age yet, but she did the advanced work," added Alexander Hilario, the director of her school, to *The Orange County Register*. "She was pretty smart."

Samantha also had all the typical dreams of a little girl.

"She used to say her name wasn't Samantha but Shirley," explained Hilario, "because she was going to be Shirley Temple. She liked to sing — the Shirley Temple thing — and she was just so friendly."

Samantha had her mind made up she would be a dancer, asking her mother if she could resume ballet lessons in the fall.

"She was always so graceful," recalled a neighbor, Theresa Rodgers. "A real little star in the making . . . She was just a sweetie. She had a smile for everybody and was so full of life."

"Samantha enjoyed herself," recalled Heidi Clifford, who also lived in the Smoketree complex. "She was a happy, bubbly little girl, doing her thing, enjoying her little life."

Despite her "Tigrita's" strength, Erin had always been concerned for little Samantha. Besides moving to a safer neighborhood, Erin taught her daughter about the perils of strangers. She knew the adorable face that brought such joy to so many could also attract trouble. The two acted out potential scenarios in their living room. Erin would play the "bad guy," trying to entice the adorable tyke into a car.

"She's cute," explained Erin. "And it always did scare me."

Mom instructed Samantha to yell "Fire!" if she was ever

Danielle van Dam (above) in a photograph taken shortly before her murder. David Westerfield took Danielle from her bedroom (right).

Brenda van Dam holds a photo of Danielle while she and her husband Damon talk about their missing daughter.

Authorities search the home of David Westerfield (above). Westerfield (right) holding a bottle of laundry detergent – one of Danielle's hairs was found in his dryer lint.

Brenda van Dam breaks down during testimony and husband Damon (far right) is consoled by John Walsh, host of *America's Most Wanted*.

Police at the desolate area where Danielle's body had been dumped.

David Westerfield (left) as Prosector Jeff Dusek (right) makes his closing arguments during the trial.

VAN DAM RESIDENCE
DYLEN'S ROOM

Brenda van Dam's friend, Denise Kemal, points to an exhibit showing photos of Dad's Cafe during Westerfield's trial.

Miranda Gaddis poses in her dance uniform – the same clothes she was wearing when she was abducted.

AP/Wide World Photos

FBI spokeswoman, Beth Anne Steele (right), displays clothes similar to those worn by Ashley Pond (above) on the day of her disappearance.

AP/Wide World Photos

A yellow ribbon marks a tree in the neighborhood where Ashley and Miranda lived.

Terri Duffey, the aunt of Miranda Gaddis, and a friend at a memorial for Ashley and Miranda.

Michelle Duffey (far left), Miranda's mother, and Lori Pond, Ashley's mother, speak to the media in front of a billboard that was donated by a local marketing firm.

FBI agents digging in the backyard of Ward Weaver III's home where both girls' bodies were found.

Ward Weaver III (right) is the suspect in the murder of Ashley Pond and Miranda Gaddis. His father, Ward F. Weaver Jr. (far right), is currently on death row for a 1981 murder.

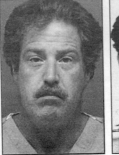 

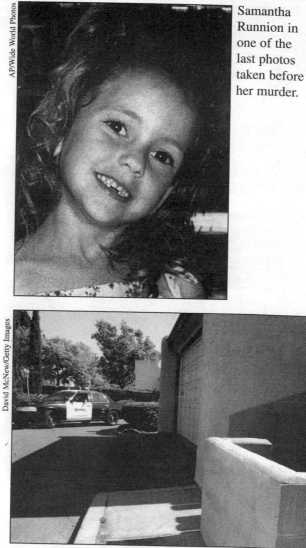

Samantha Runnion in one of the last photos taken before her murder.

Samantha was abducted as she sat on this wall at her family's condominium complex.

Derek J. Jackson (above) comments on the death of his daughter. Samantha's mother, Erin Runnion, expresses her grief as she shows two photos of her murdered daughter (right).

Investigators found Samantha's body in this rugged, heavily forested area on the edge of the Cleveland National Forest.

Sheriff Michael Carona announces at a press conference that the body of Samantha Runnion had been found.

Erin Runnion and her partner, Ken Donnelly, follow Samantha's casket during her funeral.

Alejandro Avila (left), is charged in the abduction and murder of Samantha Runnion. Beth Veglahn (right), his former fiancee, wipes away a tear while appearing on *Larry King Live*.

Mother of the accused, Adelina Avila (center) talks to reporters from the doorway of her apartment, which was searched by authorities.

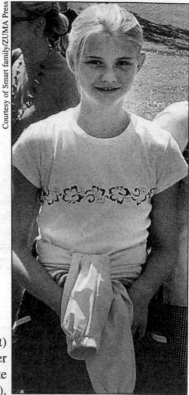

Courtesy of Smart family/ZUMA Press

Elizabeth Smart (right) was abducted from her home in Salt Lake City, Utah (below).

Scott McKiernan/ZUMA Press

Elizabeth's parents, Ed and Lois Smart, were asleep when she was taken from their home.

Sheriff's deputies prepare to search for Elizabeth.

Richard Ricci, the Smarts' former handyman, was a prime suspect in Elizabeth's disappearance. He was jailed on a probation violation before he died from a blood clot to the brain August 30, 2002.

A 1993 photo of twelve-year-old Polly Klaas of Petaluma, California. Richard Allen Davis is on death row for her murder.

Amber Hagerman, nine, of Arlington, Texas, was found dead January 17, 2002. The Amber Alert, created in her memory, has now saved over 30 other abducted children.

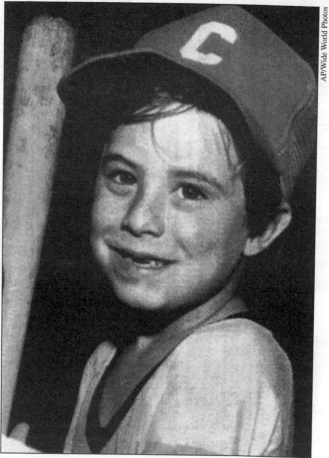

Two fishermen found the head of six-year-old Adam Walsh in a canal about 50 miles south of Vero Beach, Florida, August 12, 1981.

grabbed. Samantha, with a confident smile, said that she would get away because she "could run really fast and was as strong as Hercules."

The Greek hero with incredible strength was one of Samantha's favorite characters. She also loved Peter Pan because not only could he fly but he would never grow old. The little girl had both of their posters on the wall over her bed in the room she shared with Paige and Conner.

Samantha was about to celebrate her sixth birthday, and her parents planned a party at Goofy's Kitchen at the Disney Hotel. She had asked for a 3-D dinosaur puzzle, LEGOs, Lincoln Logs, and dresses for her Barbie.

"She asked for everything her brother got on his birthday in May," said Erin. "Plus the girl stuff."

But despite all the precautions Erin took over the years and her daughter's courageous confidence, Samantha would never celebrate that birthday.

On Monday, July 15, 2002, Samantha finished dinner at 6:30 p.m. and politely asked her grandmother, Virginia, if she could go outside. The bright-eyed girl, wearing a white blouse and red-checkered pants, walked with her friend, six-year-old Sarah Ahn, 150 feet down their road to a low brick wall on the condo complex's fringe. The two sat down and began playing the board game Clue, where participants try to solve a murder mystery.

As the girls laughed and enjoyed the warm summer evening, at about 6:45 p.m. a green two-door car drove slowly by, then turned around and pulled up alongside the wall. A man stepped out of the car and claimed to have lost his Chihuahua puppy. It was the perfect ruse, one of the oldest in the "kidnapper's handbook," as one police official described.

"How big?" Samantha asked, jumping from the wall and

leaning over to indicate a sample height with her hand.

That was when the man lunged forward and grabbed her by an arm and a leg. As little Samantha kicked and screamed as hard and loud as she could, the man threw her into his car.

In less than a minute, she was gone.

"She screamed, 'Help me! Tell my grandmother!' " Sarah Ahn recalled to an ABC reporter. "He threw her in the car really quick and he left really quick . . . The bad guy took her, but I don't know where she went."

CHAPTER 18

As soon as Virginia Runnion heard Sarah Ahn's story, she frantically dialed 911. From the moment Samantha had been abducted, her little friend did everything right, notifying adults and recalling fine details of the assailant and his car, all of which were passed on to authorities. The next call Virginia made was to her daughter, Erin, still at work.

Virginia told Erin only, "You have to come home, you have to come home," before admitting, "something has happened."

Erin fought back tears while driving from her office that Monday evening. Her first call had been to Samantha's natural father, Derek Jackson, of Sunderland, Massachusetts, hoping that he had taken their daughter. Jackson was as shocked and devastated as everyone else.

By the time the mother pulled into the Smoketree complex, a massive and unprecedented response was already underway.

Within minutes of receiving Virginia's call, the Orange County Sheriff's Department sent every available man to the scene and even called in reserves. Two police helicopters were soon in the air. Bloodhounds ran through the complex.

More than 150 personnel, including thirty FBI agents, eventually arrived.

Investigators from the Stanton division of the Orange County Sheriff's Department combed through the surrounding areas. They began a search of all of the local businesses, looking for clues and reviewing security videotapes. A flyer was produced and distributed. It had been printed in English, and was then translated into Spanish and Vietnamese, other prevalent languages in the ethnically mixed Stanton neighborhood. The files of registered sex offenders both in Orange County and across the state were being reviewed. Even Mexican law enforcement had been notified in case the abductor tried to flee across the border.

Orange County Sheriff Mike Carona, himself the father of an eleven-year-old son, took charge of the case as if he were looking for his own child. Throughout the investigation, he would present an equal dose of sensitivity with hardened resolve. Carona has a fighter's face — deep-set eyes, a nose broken three times in childhood brawls, and a disarming habit of staring people straight in the eye. He inspired confidence in victims and struck fear in criminals.

As the media inevitably descended on Stanton only a half step behind authorities, Carona elected to call upon reporters to help. Where some officials choose to keep their information to themselves, the sheriff wanted to use every tool at his disposal. A CARE, or "child abduction regional emergency," alert was announced through radio and other media outlets. Authorities also broadcast an alert on their "red channel," a nationwide communication system.

But despite all the efforts, the minutes soon ran into hours without any sign of little Samantha.

Erin and Donnelly spent the night walking and driving through town, posting flyers and desperately searching for her daughter. At one point, the mother spotted a light green car matching the description of the abductor's vehicle that Sarah Ahn had given. Erin jumped on the hood in tears and demanded that the driver open the trunk.

"I heard her in my head screaming out to me, 'Mommy!'" Erin explained, adding that the scene was repeated a few more times before the sun came up again. Some people accommodated her requests; others drove away.

By ten o'clock Tuesday morning, Erin had barely gotten thirty minutes of sleep, subsisting on little more than coffee. After roaming the streets, she and her partner had contacted every missing-child website they could think of.

"We're approaching the fifteenth hour," said Donnelly.

"With every hour, it gets worse," Erin added. "I feel very unlucky."

Their dining room table was littered with photographs. On the refrigerator was the girl's artwork, including a picture of an animal, a house, and a woman with long hair.

"I love my family more than anybody in the hole wold," she wrote under the drawing of her own happy home. "More then enyboody in the hole wold."

"It's just the worst nightmare," Erin admitted.

The mother was still placing her hopes in Samantha's cleverness, recalling a time she got lost on her bike and immediately asked some grown-ups for help. Samantha knew her telephone number and would surely call home if she could.

"Samantha, if you are watching, baby, I love you," a tearful Erin said in a televised statement that morning, hoping to appeal to any sense of compassion the kidnapper might have. "You are such a good girl. You are so clever. Please ask your captor to let you go."

What the mother didn't talk about was a horrible premonition she had had during the night. Only later would she admit to Larry King that she felt her daughter die around two o'clock that morning.

"I was instantly just freezing," Erin recalled. "I chilled . . . chattering teeth and blinding light."

At another emotional press conference later that same day, Sheriff Carona updated the world on the progress of the investigation. Despite Erin Runnion's dark vision and his own knowledge that the odds of finding her alive grew slimmer with every passing hour, he was determined to exhaust every effort to bring the little girl home.

"It is ten days from her [Samantha's] birthday. I can guarantee you that all the resources available to law enforcement and the county of Orange, the Orange County Sheriff's Department, and the FBI will be put forward to bring Samantha home before her birthday."

Carona stepped aside and Brian Donahue, the mayor of Stanton, took over at the podium. He wanted to highlight the fact that two rewards had already been posted. British Petroleum, Erin's employer, was offering $50,000 for the safe return of Samantha. The Coalition of Police & Sheriffs had added $10,000 for information leading to the arrest and conviction of the kidnapper.

"Our entire community supports the Runnion family with our thoughts and prayers," Donahue said. "It is unthinkable that anyone would come into our safe and peaceful neighborhood and do this terrible act. Rest assured that our Orange County Sheriff's Department is doing everything and will do everything possible to seek out this criminal and return Samantha to her parents."

The next to speak was Richard Garcia, the FBI special agent in charge of the case.

"Good afternoon. Thank you, Sheriff. This is a tragic event, when a five-year-old child is taken by somebody that they don't know. The FBI is here and has extended an extensive amount of assistance to the sheriff's department. We have contacted our offices throughout the country, as well as assisted in the international aspects of getting our partners in Mexico as well.

"Any information you have regarding this child, the location of the child, the suspect and such, please call it in. The information is being broadcast through the help of the media. There's a lot of people out there watching, a lot of people looking. I implore you to call. If you have cell phones out there, use them, so we can hope to bring this child back and safely returned. Thank you."

"We need your help," Carona concluded at the press conference. "We need the public's help to identify any potential witnesses, any potential leads, any potential vehicles. If you have any information, please call the Orange County Sheriff's Department . . . We will do everything in our power to see that Samantha is brought back home to her mother by her birthday. Was it a random act? Was it a planned act? I don't know. But we'll find out . . . We're confident we are going to catch the person who did this."

Thanks to Sarah Ahn, the police already had an incredibly detailed description of their suspect. He was twenty-five to forty years of age, with greased-back, straight black hair, a black mustache, and at the time of the abduction, he was wearing a powder blue button-down shirt. FBI agent Richard Garcia said Sarah Ahn was able to identify distinctive speech patterns, and as a result, investigators believed the man was also a Hispanic American.

One person watching the press conference was Beth Veglahn. The thirty-eight-year-old mother instantly recognized the suspect police were searching for. A few years beforehand, Beth and her daughter had gone through their own nightmare with the man — Alejandro Avila.

"How did you meet Mr. Avila?" talk-show host Larry King

would later ask when Veglahn appeared as a guest on his CNN program.

"Well, actually, he was the boy next door," Veglahn replied about how their romance, which spanned from August 1996 to March 1999, began. "We met through a mutual friend and she introduced me. And it took off from there."

"He lived next door?"

"Pretty much, yes."

"What kind of work was he doing at the time?"

"He wasn't working at the time at all. He was on unemployment. And he was living with his mother and sisters."

"And so you dated. Did you plan to marry?" King asked.

"Yes, we did," Veglahn answered.

"What ended it?"

"He became physically abusive . . . He just would get angry, and at the drop of a hat, he would just get angry and become violent."

"Was that the last time you saw him, or did he continue to hound you?"

"He did continue to hound me. I had moved in with my brother at the time, and he did continue to hound me. He would stalk me at my work."

"How did it finally — how did you finally get him out of your life?"

"I just wouldn't accept his phone calls. I told him to stay away from me. I put in a restraining order against him, just stayed away from him."

"Alex was the English name you used for him?"

"That's the name he uses . . . He likes to be called Alex."

"Alex Avila is how you know him . . ." King, having established the background of their relationship, launched into the subsequent development. Veglahn had experienced firsthand every parent's worst nightmare. "When, Beth, did you learn about him harming your daughter?"

"Well, it was a year . . ."

"Later?"

"Yes."

"You saw nothing while you were with him?"

"Looking at the time, no."

"How old was your daughter at this time?" King asked.

"Nine."

"She's now, like . . ."

"She's going to be twelve."

"How did you learn of it?"

"Well, it was a year later . . ." Veglahn's daughter was living with her father, Jim Coker, and called her mom on the telephone. "And at the time, I had a new boyfriend. And she [my daughter] told me that she needed to tell me something. And she went into the bathroom with the phone, because it was a cordless phone, and she told me that . . . 'I have something important to tell you.' And I said, 'Well, is it good or bad?' And she goes, 'It's bad.' And she told me that Alex had molested her."

"What did you do?" asked King.

"I told my daughter . . . I took a deep breath and I told my daughter that I loved her and everything is going to be okay, that there are some things that mommy has to do, so you need to get off the phone and mommy will call you right back."

"And what did mommy do?"

"Mommy called the sheriff's department immediately."

CHAPTER 19

Within days of Beth Veglahn's call to the sheriff, another child came forward to corroborate her daughter's story. Rosemary Drabek was Veglahn's sister, and her daughter also reported having been molested while in the care of Alejandro Avila. Now two girls, both nine at the time the abuse was alleged, were saying he had done unspeakable things. The girls, both of whose names have been changed to protect them, are Jane, Veglahn's daughter, and her cousin, Mary, Drabek's daughter. Their assertions immediately led to an extensive investigation.

On January 6 and 11, 2000, just after authorities became involved, two tape-recorded interrogations of Avila were made. In those, Avila confessed to "soaping" Jane's genitals on numerous occasions while bathing her and applying lotion to her body. On January 14, when a deputy went to Avila's work at a medical supply company to detain him, the suspect suddenly bolted out a side door. He turned himself in a week later, but only after hiring an attorney, John Pozza.

Police decided there was more than enough evidence to proceed, and a trial date was set. On Thursday, December 28, 2000, Judge Robert Spitzer and a jury of twelve men and women were ready to begin. Pozza would defend his client, who had pled not guilty to charges that included "lewd and lascivious" acts upon two separate minors. Paul Dickerson, a deputy district attorney, would prosecute for the state.

From the start, despite his eagerness to charge Avila, Dickerson knew there were challenges to the case ahead. He had, for the most part, only the testimony of two ten-year-old girls to rely upon. Their stories were shockingly detailed, but there was always the possibility that a jury might question the accuracy and memory of such young witnesses. The only physical evidence Dickerson had was a collection of pornographic videos found by investigators, none of which depicted minors, and a single printed photograph found folded up in a nightstand next to Avila's bed.

The judge described the photograph as "an eight-by-ten photograph, apparently of a female child with pigtails, eyes open, mouth open, apparently engaged in full-on sexual intercourse with a male."

Although Dickerson would use the photograph to show sexual intent when Avila touched the children, an essential component to conviction, it wasn't much. The photograph had not even been found by investigators, but rather by Rosemary Drabek after Avila had moved out of her ex-boyfriend Jose Barragan's home. The defense would argue it could have easily been planted.

Dickerson also charged Avila with making a death threat, but like the photo, the defense would argue that this could have been fabricated, also. Drabek claimed to have received a call on her cell phone while sitting in a noisy movie theater with her family just after Avila posted bail on the molestation charges. She recognized Avila as the voice that said simply, "You're dead." Drabek's boyfriend at the time, Jose Barragan, ran out to the lobby and, after seeing Avila's car in the parking lot, immediately found the pay phone the call had been made from, matching the number to the one recorded on Beth's cell phone.

Despite the tentative proof linking Avila to the child pornography and the threatening phone call, Dickerson had personally spoken with the two young victims and was confident their testimony would help take a sick pedophile off the streets.

"You are going to hear when she [Veglahn] would go to work, the defendant got to baby-sit her [Jane]." Dickerson began. "And that's why I think this is the ultimate violation of trust . . .

"The defendant would French kiss her, made her watch pornographic movies. He bathed and touched her naked body, meaning her vagina and her breasts and her bottom; that he rubbed his penis on her vagina . . . That he also placed small plastic tubes in her vagina.

"They would be in the bedroom, and Jane would try to wiggle away and he [Avila] would grab her and he would hold her mouth, 'Come back here, because I want to keep touching you.' That's force. It's more force than you would need . . . He would tell her, 'Look, if you tell anybody, I am going to hurt your mother or I am going to kill you or kill your family.' "

Regarding the allegations made by Jane's cousin Mary, the prosecutor said, "He [Avila] would rub on her chest . . . and that he would also rub her vagina. The conduct is not as serious, but still you are going to hear that he rubbed her vagina and rubbed her breasts."

Discussing Avila's own admissions on the interrogation tapes, "You are going to hear 'I did wash Jane's vagina with soap twelve times. I washed her buttocks' — and I think you are going to hear he is going to say 'where she couldn't reach.' And she is nine. 'I washed her breasts.' "

Avila's attorney, John Pozza, had his turn to address the jury later that same day. His job was to convince them that the witnesses, on whom the entire trial would hinge, should be doubted. The burden of proof fell to the prosecution, and Pozza would do whatever he could to minimize that proof.

"I don't believe there will be any physical evidence of any kind of this alleged conduct, no medical reports, no counselor reports, no psychologist reports. At some point she [Jane] had a friend and she spoke with this friend and this friend advised her that she had been molested by her uncle. Now, I don't know the full context of their conversation, because I haven't talked to Jane, but there is a report . . . Shortly after speaking with this friend, she [Jane] contacts her cousin Mary . . . And all of a sudden these allegations arise.

"Their statements have not been consistent . . . While you are listening to them, is their testimony consistent? Is it plausible? Could innocent conduct be misconstrued? Have they been coached? Have they been influenced by other events? Was there actual force used?

"Being charged as a child molester has got to be the worst thing that could happen to any member of our society," concluded the defense attorney. "Murder, robbery, arson, don't conjure up the same knee-jerk reaction of disgust that this allegation does . . . Carefully listen to the testimony, and keep an open mind. That is the true calling of an American jury."

With that, both sides had made their opening arguments

in the case of the *State of California v. Alejandro Avila*. The defendant's future would soon be in the hands of a jury consisting of twelve of his peers, empowered to judge both sides and find guilt or innocence.

Little did any of the jurors know then that ultimately another life would also be tragically affected by their verdict.

CHAPTER 20

The first witness called by the prosecution was the girl who had originally made the allegations against Avila, Jane Veglahn. The judge, after asking Jane to remove her chewing gum, urged her to try to recall the facts as best she could. He, for one, understood that testimony from a child was never as definitive as that from an adult witness. Jane's mother, Beth Veglahn, sat nervously nearby. Alejandro Avila stared at the girl from the defense table.

"How old are you, Jane?" Dickerson began.

"Ten," Jane replied.

"What grade are you in?"

"Fifth."

"Fifth? What's you favorite subject?"

"I like language, writing stories."

"What kind of stories do you like to write?"

"Sometimes like fantasy stories."

"Fantasy stories?" Dickerson asked.

Jane nodded her head up and down, and the prosecutor quickly elected to move on to more serious questions. "Did the defendant ever put his hands on you in a way that bothered you? Did he ever touch you?"

"Yes he did," replied Jane.

"Why don't you tell the jury what the defendant — how the defendant would touch you and what he did."

"What he would do is he would touch down by my private area and rub like his fingers around there."

"And what else did he do?"

"And he would also rub — like take his private part and rub it around mine, my area, private part."

"When he would do this, did you have underwear on?"
"No."

"Okay. Would you have a shirt on?"

"No. I would have no clothes on . . . When he would be doing that with his private part, he wouldn't be wearing anything either."

"Did he ever — did he ever kiss you?"

"Yes, he would kiss me on my mouth."

"Would he ever kiss you with his tongue?"
"Yes."

"Did he ever touch your chest?"
"Yes."

"Could you tell me the circumstances? Do you understand my question? How did it happen?"

"When my mom went to work, he would take me into the room and he would do those things to me . . . And he would shut the door and lock it so my brothers wouldn't come in."

"Where would your brothers be?"

"Out in the living room watching TV or playing with each other, playing video games."

"How would you react when the defendant would be touching you?"

"I was scared, and I was just hoping it would be over soon."

"Did you ever — did you ever try to get away?"

"Yes . . . I would try and go away. And he would put his hand over my mouth and jerk me and say, 'Don't go. Don't move.' "

"Did he ever — were you ever in the bathroom with him?"

"He would make me take showers with him . . . He would make me wash him and then he would wash me."

"Did you ever touch the defendant when you were in the bathroom?"

"He would make me, like, kiss his private part . . . Like, when, like, after he would wash me he would make me wash him. He would, like, when we were still in the shower, he would make me kiss his private part."

Then the two discussed in detail one of the most egregious stories of all — how Avila had inserted small plastic tubes into the girl. According to Jane, after Avila had done it to her repeatedly, he instructed her to do it herself while he watched.

"Did he ever put anything inside your body?" Dickerson asked the girl.

"Yes."

"Okay. What?"

"It would be like these little plastic tubes that he got from his work, because he worked at this place where they would ship medical supplies to hospitals."

"Okay."

"The first time he showed me what to do, he would put it in . . . and he would push it in and out and he would say 'practice' and make me do that."

"Did he ever show you any kind of — any movies?"

"Yes."

"What kind of movies did he show you?"

"Men and women doing that . . . Doing sort of like the things he was doing to me."

"You said you are in fifth grade, right?"

"Yes."

"Now, this happened to you when you were in fourth grade?"

"Third."

"Is there a reason that you didn't tell your mom about what was going on?"

"Because when he did this to me, I got scared. And one time he threatened me and he said, 'I would kill your mom or hurt your family' . . . I believed him."

After Dickerson finished with his first witness, Pozza rose from the defense table next to Avila and approached the girl. He intended to pepper her with many of the same questions about minute details, inevitably bringing out inconsistencies in her testimony. He also had a few key points in mind to touch upon.

"Do you like writing stories?" asked Pozza, following up on her earlier admission to Dickerson.

"Yeah," Jane replied.

"Okay. You like performing?"

"Yes."

"Acting?"

"A little bit."

"Okay," Pozza was ready to move on. "So, the whole time you were in the room, you and Alex were both naked?"

"Yes."

"For that entire two hours, three hours?"

"Yes."

"And the whole time that you were in the room for the two to three hours, Alex was touching you?"

"Yes."

"Did you ever shout out to your brothers?"

"No."

"Did you ever make any noises in the room?"

"No."

"Now, do you have a little friend named Stephanie in Orange County?"

"Yes."

"And how do you know Stephanie?"

"When we went to school . . . we were in the same class and we became friends."

"Now, did Stephanie ever tell you that she had been touched?"

"Yes."

"When did she tell you that?"

"I don't know. I don't remember. I don't remember."

"Was it before you told people that Alex had touched you?"

"Yes . . . That I remember, maybe, I don't know, I don't remember, maybe."

As Pozza returned to his seat and Jane was dismissed, Dickerson called his next witness — Jane's cousin Mary. Once again, the judge primed the witness to be truthful and to do the best that she could under the tough circumstances. Mary's mother sat close by for support as the victim faced Avila. After a few questions about her date of birth and favorite subjects in school, Dickerson began the real questioning.

"While he was baby-sitting you, did he ever touch you in a way that you didn't like?" he asked.

"In my private area."

"What would he do? Would he touch you over your clothes or under your clothes?"

"Under."

"Okay. How many times do you think he touched your private parts?"

"Twice."

"Was this when you were in fourth grade?"

"Third."

"Why don't you tell me what happened when — the first time when he touched you?"

"He put his finger in my private area and started moving his finger really fast."

"Were you wearing clothes?"

"Yes."

"Did he — so he reached his hand underneath your clothes?"

"Yes."

"Did he say anything to you after he touched your private part?"

"He said, 'It's our secret. Don't tell.' "

Later, Dickerson would lead the witness to the second occasion she recalled Avila molesting her. According to both girls, there had been a time where Avila brazenly touched them when all three were in the same room at Beth Veglahn's apartment.

"We were all just sitting next to each other," Mary recalled. "And he did that. He did that to me and Jane."

"You said you were sitting on a bed?"

"Yes."

"Okay. And your cousin was on the bed?"

"Yes."

"And you said he touched you there?"

"Yes."

"Did he reach under your underwear?"

"Yes."

When Pozza got his own turn with Mary, he immediately went to the same incident. The very brazenness that Dickerson tried to highlight could also be used to discount whether the incident actually happened. Pozza also wanted to raise another question typically asked in such cases: Why would someone allow something like this to be done to them and, even more, not tell anyone? Essentially the goal was to lay blame on the victim.

"Now, while he is doing this, what were you doing?" Pozza began.

"We were just watching TV," Mary replied.

"So it didn't bother you that he started unsnapping your clothes. You didn't say, 'Stop, Alex.'"

"No."

"And now he unbuttoned — unsnapped your clothes and then you had underwear on?"

"Yes."

"And then he went under your underwear?"

"Yes."

"Did you say anything to him then?"

"No."

"You just kept watching TV?"

"Yeah."

"So you are watching TV. Did you say anything to Jane?"

"No."

"Did Jane say — did she see Alex doing what he was doing?"

"Yep."

"Did she say anything?"

"No."

"Did you ever talk to your mom [about this]?"

"No."

"How about your dad?"

"No."

The gut-wrenching testimony of the victims was finally over. Dickerson had effectively guided the girls through their testimony, covering every detail of their specific charges. Pozza, on the other hand, had managed to demonstrate the tentative nature of using ten-year-olds as primary witnesses — it was often easier for adults to discount them than to trust them.

Later in the trial, Beth Veglahn would be called to the stand. The prosecution wanted to know about how Avila would treat Jane when the mother was around.

"Did you ever see him buy her things?" Dickerson asked.

"Yes."

"What would he buy her?"

"Clothes, pink crystal diamond earrings, which I thought were a little bit too elaborate, but pretty much anything she wanted."

"How did he treat your boys?"

"He didn't treat my boys very good at all."

Pozza was interested in exploring other issues with Veglahn. The alleged abuse had occurred at Veghlan's apartment while she and Avila were living together in 1999. The single mom had asked her boyfriend to baby-sit while she worked evenings. Primarily the children were living with their father, Jim Coker, during this time.

"So, while you were at [the apartment]," Pozza began his questioning. "They [the kids] went to Orange County with their father?"

"Yes."

"And was that a change of custody?"

"Yes."

"Was it an agreement or was it a court-ordered change?"

"Court-ordered."

"And what was the reason for the change?"

"Because I thought it would be in the best interests of my children if they were with their father."

Pozza soon artfully managed to ask Veglahn if she was, in fact, a recovering drug addict before Dickerson could object. Pozza then settled for launching into an assault on how the mother failed to recall the names of certain key people, as if that meant she might not have cared about her kids as a loving mother would.

"Did she [Jane] get a medical exam?"

"Yes, she did get a medical exam."

"And who arranged that exam?"

"I believe it was her counselor."

"What was that counselor's name?"

"I don't remember."

"And do you know the name of the doctor who examined Jane?"

"I don't remember."

"Did you ever tell the investigating officers about the counselor?"

"Why would I do that?" snapped Veglahn.

"It's just a question . . ." Pozza replied.

Slowly but surely, the defense attorney managed to divert the attention from Avila and the hideous crimes he had allegedly committed against two innocent little girls. Pozza even randomly asked Veglahn on the stand if she had ever "caught Jane masturbating." Although the answer came back a definitive "no," it was one more attempt to smear the accusers rather than the accused.

The seeds of doubt had been planted in the jury.

CHAPTER 21

Other witnesses called to testify during the proceedings included Avila's mother, Adelina, and his sister Elvira. Both claimed they never saw Avila engage in any inappropriate conduct with his girlfriend's children or anyone else.

A Riverside County sheriff's deputy, Victoria Carver, and Avila's former boss at the medical supply warehouse where he had worked, Jerry Constable, testified about the day Avila fled to avoid arrest. His boss went to get Avila from a warehouse while the deputy waited in a reception area. As Avila and Constable walked back together, Avila grew more and more agitated, before suddenly running out a side door. By this point he had been questioned twice and obviously knew he was in some serious trouble.

"I walked back up into my office and basically told him that the deputies were up front and that he needed to go up there with me," recalled Constable when prompted by Dickerson. "And he kind of made a statement of, 'I've got to get out of here. I've got to go.' Or something, and took off running down the stairs and at that point left out a back entrance."

To counter the incriminating flight, Pozza would argue that Avila had already submitted voluntarily to two previous interviews and may have simply been feeling the duress of such serious charges. Pozza then moved on to his character witnesses. Adelina, Avila's mother, had spent time in Beth and Avila's apartment while her son baby-sat.

"Now, while they [Jane and her brothers] were at the house, were you also at the apartment?" Pozza asked.

"Yes, I was," Adelina replied.

"And you know those children fairly well?"

"They're pretty friendly."

"Did the children ever appear to be afraid of Alex?"

"No."

"You said you have six children?"

"Yes."

"And you've raised all of those children?"

"Yes, I did."

"And you believe if you had observed anything inappropriate in the house, you would have known it?"

"Yes, I would."

Next to be called to the witness stand was Avila's sister, Elvira, who had also spent time in Veglahn's apartment.

"While you were at the apartment . . . did you ever see Alex do anything inappropriately with children?"

"No."

"How would you describe his interactions with the children? Did they get along with him? Was he friendly?"

"Yeah, he got along with them."

"It was a small apartment, correct?"

"Yeah."

"Pretty close quarters?"

"It's a one-bedroom."

Some of the most damning evidence against Avila came toward the end of the trial, when prosecutors played the interrogation tapes authorities had made when they first questioned Avila. In them, the defendant detailed how when he baby-sat he made a point of bathing Jane and meticulously applying soap and lotion to her body. At one point he said he may have "touched her vagina once or twice," and then on another he acknowledged that number might have been "twelve times."

By Wednesday, January 3, 2001, both sides were ready to make their closing arguments, and Deputy District Attorney Dickerson rose first to address the twelve members of the jury.

"Thank you, everybody, for being patient," began the prosecutor. "I'll try to get through this as quickly as I can . . . Now, I hope that I'm not being too elementary when I try to explain this, but this is actually the way I walked through it myself. I'm sorry if it seems too simple, but this is actually how I do it.

"Your job in this case is going to be to decide these issues, and how are you going to decide the issues? One, you have to decide what the facts are from the statements that you heard from the witnesses . . . He [Avila] fondled Jane's vagina . . . She said he fondled her breasts. She said he rubbed his penis on her vagina. She sucked his penis. She touched the penis. He placed tubes in the vagina.

"The defendant admitted [on the interrogation tape] that he touched Jane. He said 'I touched her vagina twelve times in the bathroom.' He admits to touching her breasts. Again, that's in the tape. He also admits to touching her vagina six times in the living room and that she was in her underwear . . . So you have corroborating evidence of what Jane sat up there and told you . . .

"How do you infer specific intent, what his intent was when he touched her? I believe if you take a nine-year-old girl who is naked alone in the bathtub and you take soap on your hands and you reached under her legs and you rub lotion on her vagina . . . there is only one reasonable conclusion that you can find, and that he was doing it to satisfy his lust, his sexual desires for this young girl.

"My favorite statement that defense counsel made [was] 'What's the harm in bathing Jane?' Well, she wasn't three . . . she was eight. An eight-year-old child can wash herself. There is no reason for a boyfriend when mommy is not home to put the child in the tub naked, put soap on his hands, and wash her vagina or wash her bottom or wash her breasts. She can do it herself. You saw her — she's not injured. She's not a paraplegic. Why don't you go in and take a bath just to clean up. He didn't need to do it. He violated her. That's why he touched her.

"I also put down here the strength of the testimony given her age. I think she did a pretty darn good job, given how old she was. You think about this for a second. Here's a ten-year-old who is going to get up in front of strangers who are staring at her, in front of a judge who is staring at her . . . and then she has to go through the humiliation of cross-examination from a defense attorney. Now, you tell me if that little child didn't do a good job . . .

"So what is the conclusion that I believe you need to reach with this defendant? The defendant molested [these girls]. That's what he did; that's what you should find. Don't let him get away with this . . . I'm asking you to hold him responsible for what he did to those little children . . . Don't let him get away with this. Do not let him get away with this. Please come back with verdicts of guilty on all counts."

After thanking the judge and jury, Dickerson stepped away and returned to the prosecutor's table. Pozza, after giving Avila a reassuring look, rose to address the court. Dickerson had done a good job, but he felt he could do better.

"Good morning, ladies and gentlemen of the jury. First of all, on behalf of Mr. Avila and myself, I would like to thank you for the time and attention you've given this case. I know it hasn't been the easiest case to sit through and listen to. The mere allegation is enough to make most people have a knee-jerk reaction and say, 'Wow, that's incredible, this guy is a monster.'

"But what we need to do is really look at things, and that's what I've tried to do when we've had witnesses up on the stand, try to elicit information so we know exactly what is going on and so that when you are deliberating, you can go through each necessary element and say has this been proved beyond a reasonable doubt or is there some doubt as to the authenticity or truthfulness of the testimony that you've heard?

"First, I'd like to discuss Jane's testimony. Certainly, the prosecution is correct, that it cannot be easy for a ten-year-old to get up on the stand in front of strangers and talk about something — allegations which are so heinous — but we had Jane on the stand. We all saw her. We all observed her. It did not appear she had a lot of trouble telling you what her story was.

"And what did we find out? We found out that the allegations were made after a friend of hers in Orange County had made similar allegations against her uncle . . . She also testified that when she was alone with Alex she was in the bedroom with the door shut for two to three hours. Her brothers were outside. According to Jane, this happened maybe fifty times during that one year . . . There's a problem with reality there, ladies and gentlemen. You've got two older brothers who are outside — allegedly outside the bedroom with the door closed, and this is occurring — the allegations can't be in a vacuum.

"Now, is it possible, is it conceivable that these two boys

know that their sister is in the bedroom with Alex, the door closed, and this happens every weekend and she's in there for two to three hours? Is it conceivable that these two boys would not have mentioned something? But you have to ask yourself, is it conceivable? We're dealing with a one-bedroom apartment, a whole issue of people living there. This is not some cabin in the woods, where, you know, it's secluded, where two to three hours can pass and no one knows what's going on.

"Then the fact that during this whole time period she didn't tell anyone. Is it totally conceivable that this could be going on in this one-bedroom apartment — brothers, cousins, aunts, a mother, everybody there, but no one knows about it, and she's afraid to tell? You have to ask yourself that.

"It's very easy to get caught up in the fact that this young girl is saying these things, saying stuff that is horrible, that is outrageous, this guy is a monster, but you have to look at the specific little things that come out, and those are the things that are telling you what would make her say that? Was she coached? Has she been exposed to something else? We don't know. But certainly that should lead to some doubt. That should lead to some doubt.

"Then we get to Alex's interview. Fortunately the transcript and the tape are in evidence, so you can review that. Now, in reviewing that, again, don't look at it very quickly. I want you to look at it and make sure that things are not taken out of context. Okay? Because it's very important. Mr. Dickerson is saying he's admitted this, he admitted it, he's guilty. If you listen to the tape, he admitted to touching her vagina with soap while bathing . . . There's no crime to giving someone a bath and possibly touching them with soap . . . You have to touch them with sexual intent, and that's what has to be proved here.

"Mr. Dickerson told you he wasn't sure in his opening what these kids were going to say. He wasn't sure. He couldn't tell you exactly what they were going to say until they got up there and said it. Why is that? Is it because the story kept changing and Mr. Dickerson just wanted to wait until they got up on the stand and see what they're going to say and he'd argue that point? Is that what happened here?

"We heard absolutely no evidence of Alex's past, nothing to indicate that he's a volatile, violent person . . . The prosecution has to prove to you beyond a reasonable doubt that he did this. I'm just raising these questions because these are the things you as a jury have to go through and you have to come to conclusions. You have to look at the facts . . . They [the prosecution] have the burden. Like I said, I don't have to prove any of this. They have the burden to prove all of that to you beyond a reasonable doubt.

"Look at everything. It's very important. This is this guy's life. This is very important. So you have to take this job very seriously, because you've been given one of the greatest powers that a group of people can have, and that is to determine the outcome and life of a fellow citizen. That has to be taken very seriously, and that's what I ask you to do."

The jurors, having been sequestered during their deliberations, returned to the courtroom with their ruling. Pozza had led them to believe their decision would only affect his client, but the young victims and their families certainly would have argued otherwise. And in a few short years, this outcome would also have grave consequences for another little girl.

The foreman of the jury announced the unanimous verdict: "Not guilty."

Moments later, as an elated Alejandro Avila celebrated with his mother, sister, and attorney, the judge who heard the case felt a need to speak up. He, for one, knew that the jury had just made a very costly mistake.

"Your life would be totally destroyed were you convicted of an offense like this," Judge Spitzer told Avila after the jurors had been cleared from the courtroom. "So you should change your lifestyle to avoid these kinds of accusations in the future."

That warning would be ignored.

CHAPTER 22

At 3:17 p.m. on Tuesday, July 16, 2002, less than twenty-four hours after Samantha Runnion was abducted from the Smoketree Condominiums, a 911 call came in to authorities. A body had been found just off the Ortega Highway in the Cleveland National Forest. The location was fifty miles from Samantha Runnion's home, but only ten miles from where Alejandro Avila lived with his mother.

"Oh my God, I found a dead body," screamed the caller to an emergency operator. "Please hurry. Okay? I'm in the Ortegas, Okay? Ortega mountains. I'm in Riverside County, okay? Listen to me, I'm scared to sit here, there's another truck up the street and we want to get out of here. We're scared."

"I understand that," the operator tried to calm the man down. "We have to know what street."

"I'm on Killen Trail. It's a main street, there is another main street, but the big street out here, K-I-L-L-E-N Trail."

"Okay, and what is you name?"

"My name is Justin . . . Hey, can I go to my house? I'm

really nervous right now . . . Hey, we're gonna go. I'm just scared right now."

"Justin, what is your address?"

"I don't know my address there. I just moved in there, like, a couple weeks ago with my friends."

"Justin, Justin, we need you to calm down a little . . . Justin, I understand, but you need to calm down a little. Where is the body at on Killen?"

"Okay . . . I'm so scared, it was a little kid. I'm sorry."

"Calm down."

"I'm sorry but I have a three-year-old son."

"You have a three-year-old son with you? Justin, hey, hey was it an adult? Was it an adult's body?"

"It's a baby. I think it may even be the little girl that's been on the news. It's a little girl . . . I'm freaking out. I'm sorry, I'll stop, all right?"

"That's okay, that's okay."

"I'm freaking out, man. I'm sorry, but this is the scariest [expletive] thing I've ever witnessed in my life, okay?"

The minute Carona learned of the discovery, he rushed to the scene. Because the body was found in Riverside County, Carona knew that his jurisdiction as sheriff of Orange County, where the abduction originally occurred, could be compromised. Carona appealed to Riverside officials to allow him to retain his leading role, which they agreed to. Authorities wanted only to see justice done, and there was no time for internal fighting or turf wars.

By Wednesday morning, everyone's worst fears were confirmed. Samantha's grandmother identified the girl's remains through photos from the site where the body was found. Worse yct, a medical examiner revealed that she had been sexually assaulted and died of asphyxiation during her last hours. There were signs that showed the curly-haired child had fought desperately for her life before she was suffocated.

Where Carona had pledged to bring Samantha home by her birthday, now he was left to promise to find Samantha's killer. He knew, at least, that authorities had found "significant" DNA evidence at the scene of the crime. It was barely a bright spot, but that evidence could help in finding and prosecuting the assailant.

"The description of our suspect as an animal is right on point," Carona said to CNN. "I will tell you that he acted impulsively and in doing so he left a lot of evidence at the crime scene in Stanton, where the kidnap took place. He also left a lot of physical evidence for us at the crime scene where Samantha was murdered in Riverside County.

"We have collected all of that. We're working with our forensic laboratory here in Orange County and our counterparts with the FBI. We're digesting all of it, but we're very excited about what we've come across and we believe that's going to help us put the puzzle together and bring this man to justice."

In a press conference, the sheriff also had to make a much harder admission to the public.

"The way the body was found," he said, "the fact it was not buried, not hidden and such, and how it was left is almost like a calling card, like a challenge: 'I'm here and I'm coming back again.

"Based upon the behavioral profile that we've been able to get from the FBI, this person would react again within the next twenty-four hours, and so we're asking the public to be very, very cautious."

The truth was that what investigators found in the Cleveland National Forest had chilled them to the bone. Samantha's nude body had been horrifically displayed spread-eagle, brazenly left in a manner as if to taunt investigators. Forensic psychologists knew exactly what that meant — Samantha Runnion's killer intended to strike again, and soon.

That warning only infuriated and motivated investigators further.

FBI special agent in charge Garcia directly addressed the unknown killer, saying, "We will find you and we will bring you to justice."

"Don't sleep, don't eat," added Corona. "Because we're coming after you."

Over the course of the next twenty-four hours, authorities fielded thousands of tips, ranging from matching descriptions of green cars to suspicious behaviors of strangers. Other unsolved child killings nationwide were being reviewed to see if there might have been a connection. In all, some 100,000 officers throughout the country had been alerted.

In Southern California, nearly one hundred FBI agents joined about four hundred Orange County sheriff's deputies and local police officers. Governor Gray Davis added to the previously publicized rewards by offering $50,000 more for information leading to an arrest and conviction of the girl's killer. Even the White House had called to offer assistance and condolences.

Orange County Assistant Sheriff George Jaramillo discussed the manhunt with Brian Williams on CNBC.

"Could you give us the very latest?" asked the news-show host.

"What's going on is everybody in law enforcement throughout the state and frankly throughout the nation is focusing on the color of the car, the description of the potential suspect. Consequently, we've got contact with a lot of people. We're making a lot of stops. We're impounding some vehicles, and we're making other arrests that may or may not be related to this incident. We are confident that we're going to catch the monster that committed this crime."

"This is an intense local tragedy," commented Williams. "It is a huge statewide tragedy in California. Why should people in a national audience, though, listen up and pay attention to this story and take something away from it?"

"This is beyond just local tragedy. This strikes at the very heart of our freedoms and at the very heart of what we enjoy here in America, the ability to have our children grow up free, not only from crime but from this horrific type of attack. This, if you're a father, if you're a mother, if you're a child . . . we all should feel violated by what this horrible individual has perpetrated not only against the family and the child but against the society at large."

Meanwhile, outside Samantha's home a memorial spontaneously grew. Fourteen tables in the courtyard of the Smoketree complex were piled high with flowers, stuffed animals, balloons, candles, and personal messages left in English and Spanish and German. Parents and children alike, many in tears, added to the collection, trying to make sense of the tragedy.

But other than the activity around the memorial, there was a noticeable lull on the usually active grounds. Kids, typically free to run around, were quickly shuffled back inside. A nearby park was deserted. The jungle gym and swings sat empty. Everyone's sense of security had been robbed.

Erin Runnion and her family were in their apartment, trying to cope with the loss. Another grieving mother, Brenda van Dam, called and offered her condolences. It had been only a few months since her family went through the same thing.

"They were both sweet, wonderful girls who loved life and their family," Brenda said in a statement.

"Please watch your children every second; don't let them out of your sight, especially now," Derek Jackson, Samantha's natural father, told reporters outside his home in Western Massachusetts.

"I will always stay connected with her. She will live in my heart," Jackson said. "When I wake up every day I will think of her and I will think of her when I go to bed at night. I miss you, Samantha."

CHAPTER 23

As police continued to follow any and every lead, there was one that appeared to be especially promising — Beth Veglahn's. Authorities learned that not only had Avila barely escaped a long prison sentence but he was also familiar with the Smoketree condo complex where Samantha had been abducted. Veglahn's ex-husband, Jim Coker, had lived there, and it was the very complex where Avila had picked up Jane many times to drive her to Lake Elsinore for visits with her mother.

Then a second tip came in. Emeline Ricalde, the manager of the low-income housing complex in Lake Elsinore where Avila lived with his mother, said she saw him cleaning and inspecting his light green car on Tuesday. The color of the vehicle matched the description Sarah Ahn had given, and Avila was so meticulous about the job that Ricalde had grown suspicious that he might be trying to get rid of evidence.

Corona's decision to appeal to the public for help, coupled with Sarah Ahn's precise description of the suspect and his vehicle, had all paid off.

At 6 a.m. on Thursday, July 18, police arrived at Alejandro Avila's apartment. Avila was detained and taken to a nearby hotel where a scratch on his leg, possibly inflicted by Samantha during a struggle, was photographed. He was also interrogated for hours. At the same time, other investigators served a search warrant on his residence, combing over everything to collect any evidence.

It didn't take long to realize that Avila had a less than airtight alibi. Apparently, he was expected home Monday night to cook a chicken dinner but failed to show up. His sister Elvira later told *The Orange County Register* that Avila eventually called to say he was "just driving around" and stopped to call from the Ontario Mall. However, the sound of a plane could be heard in the background, and the Ontario Mall was an indoor shopping center.

By Friday morning, Alejandro Avila was arrested.

"I am one hundred percent certain that Mr. Avila is the man who kidnapped and murdered Samantha Runnion," Carona said during a news conference late Friday. The sheriff credited the speedy arrest to solid forensic and scientific evidence obtained from the crime scene that linked Avila to Samantha Runnion. He also described "helpful tips" from the public, facilitated by the media's effective work in spreading news of the abduction and the suspect's description.

The *Los Angeles Times*, citing police sources it did not identify, reported that DNA taken from the girl's body matched that of Alejandro Avila. In an interview with the *Times* before his Friday morning arrest, while denying any involvement in the crime, Avila did acknowledge that detectives told him they had found fibers under Samantha's fingernails linking him to her.

"This is a message from me on behalf of Samantha's family to Mr. Alejandro Avila," announced Carona. "What you didn't realize [is that] when we found Samantha's body and this investigation took place, Samantha became our little girl."

By the time a memorial service was held on Wednesday, July 24, more than three thousand people packed into the Crystal Cathedral in Garden Grove, California. Thousands more stood outside to pay their respects, while millions watched at home as CNN broadcast the funeral live. A skywriter drew hearts and Samantha's initials overhead in a clear sky.

The cathedral was adorned with pink and white roses. A purple candle flickered as a centerpiece on the altar. A bouquet of roses covered the tiny casket that held Samantha's body. Two children's choirs performed in turn. An orchestra later played the song "I Can Fly" from Peter Pan.

The pastor of the church, Dr. Robert Schuller, a nationally known television evangelist, began the somber ceremony.

"Today, when I look over this sea of people, and I see the crowds standing outside . . . I see where truth is. I see the love that is in this community, because today, this is a symbol of the love and the support for this family. As evil has taken place and has robbed them of life, and today we mourn because it's not fair. It's not fair that we're looking at a tiny little casket . . .

"But what is right, what is true, and what is good is what brought all of you here today. A love, a support, a community. Tragedy brings us together, yes. But we'll triumph through it . . . That the message might be proclaimed, that evil might be overcome with love."

The next to speak at the gathering was Sheriff Mike Carona. During the investigation, he had proven to be a solid and responsible representative of the law. But when he spoke of his bond with the little girl he had never met and her family, the sincere compassion of a father came through.

"Samantha was a little girl. Little girls aren't supposed to die. Little girls aren't supposed to die the way Samantha died . . . It's Tuesday afternoon, July the sixteenth, the first time that I met Samantha's mom. Erin and I talked specifically and hopefully about bringing Samantha home. Erin gave me a picture of Samantha. A big smile, curly hair, big brown eyes. And I promised her that I would keep the picture next to me until we brought Samantha home.

"On July nineteenth, I sat down with Erin to tell her that we made an arrest on the man that had murdered her daughter. I tried to give her back the photograph that she had given me that Tuesday afternoon. Erin wouldn't take the picture. She told me that Samantha would want me to keep it.

"This Monday, Erin sent over to my office a stuffed animal, a little tiger. And she wanted me to keep it because it was Samantha's favorite stuffed animal. She kept it on her bed, slept with it. And Erin wanted to make sure that I had that so I could always remember Samantha.

"I didn't need a picture. And I didn't need a stuffed animal to remember Samantha. I told you all before, Samantha was our little girl. Samantha is our little girl. For those of us who are involved in this investigation, the Orange County Sheriff's Department, and the Federal Bureau of Investigation, Riverside County Sheriff's Department, California Highway Patrol, and the countless volunteers that were all out there, Samantha was our little girl.

"We loved her dearly. And there was a passion to find her killer. Erin took the time to come out to the command post. And I think she got it firsthand what we were talking about. The incredible passion, men and women who literally had to be ordered to go home, because they didn't want to give up in the search, who were sleeping in their cars for a couple hours, only to come back and to do it all again.

"To grab tip sheets and to get out in the field. To serve coffee to those that were working. The media, who never left our sides and kept the message out there in the public. And the public, who were constantly working with us to catch Samantha's killer.

"We didn't realize it at the time, but Samantha was not just our little girl, she became America's little girl. Samantha was all that was good in the world. And what happened to her is all that was evil in the world. When we arrested the individual that murdered Samantha, all of us in the command post rejoiced that he was captured before another child was injured.

"But we're struggling with an incredible sadness that overcame all of us who have been part of this investigation because we wanted to bring Samantha home, and all that we did, for all the magnificent work that was done, by hundreds of men and women who are true professionals, we couldn't bring Samantha back.

"Late Friday night, I was sitting in the command post, and I was talking with Sandy Hill with the Trauma Intervention Program, who was assigned to Samantha's little friend Sarah. And I was curious how Sarah was doing through all of this and if she missed her little friend.

"Sandy said, 'Sheriff, I've got to tell you a story about Sarah. I asked Sarah this morning if she missed Samantha. She said, 'I miss her a lot, but I'm not sad anymore because Samantha is home with Jesus in heaven.' "

Finally, Erin Runnion stepped to the microphone. Her eyes were tired and red, her face pale and drawn. It had been only ten days since she received that frantic call from her mother begging her to come home right away. Those ten days felt like ten years. In a tribute to her daughter's lively spirit, Erin wore red rather than black at the funeral.

"Thank you all for coming. This has been the most awful nightmare, and your sympathy and love throughout have given my family tremendous comfort and strength . . . We are overwhelmed by the love people have shown Samantha . . . And that is why we felt compelled to share this memorial with everyone whose heart has been touched by her death.

"Ken and I were truly honored to be her parents. We always knew she had a gift for the world, but it never occurred to us that her greatness would be realized in her death . . . May everyone be inspired by her joy and take comfort in the gift that is every child. May our nation take this tragedy and unite in the protection and wonderment of all children."

CHAPTER 24

As the weeks passed after Samantha's memorial, Erin Runnion's final words hung on the consciousness of many who had been touched by the tragedy of her daughter's death. As an uneasy routine returned, some couldn't help but wonder about the man responsible. Erin Runnion had called on everyone to be concerned with the welfare of children. But hadn't Alejandro Avila once appeared to do exactly that?

How did "the boy next door," as Beth Veglahn once described Avila, become the monster responsible for so much pain? Through a look at his past, warning signs emerge, but the friendly neighbor always managed to earn the trust of unsuspecting parents.

To the many harried single moms who inhabited Avila's Lake Elsinore apartment complex in the mid 1990s, Avila had, in fact, seemed like a godsend. In this blue-collar community eighty miles southeast of Los Angeles, many struggling parents worked odd jobs at odd hours for low pay, and they couldn't always afford pricey day-care centers or baby-sitters.

On hot summer days, when temperatures hovered in the nineties for weeks on end, perhaps a dozen children might be playing in the backyard's scorched grass or splashing around in the outdoor pool. For the busy moms, it was always nice to know that Alex, as he liked to be called, had time on his hands and didn't seem to mind sitting out in the searing heat, watching the kids.

Neighbors noticed that Alex, then in his early twenties, didn't drink or curse like so many of the rap-music generation, and he seemed to have endless patience for even the silliest children's games and banter. As one of his former neighbors put it, "Alex could be incredibly sweet, gentle, and personable. He totally gained my trust, as well as the love and trust of my three-year-old daughter."

The neighbor, after all, considered herself a pretty good judge of character. She'd worked for the California Department of Corrections for almost twenty years at the time, and she'd seen all manner of criminals and con men, even sex offenders, but Alex seemed nothing like them. She so trusted the mild-mannered Avila, and he seemed so good with children that she gave him the run of her apartment and happily let him baby-sit her little girl.

"I was a working mom, and when I needed a baby-sitter, Alex offered immediately. He was a friend and, since he lived upstairs, it was convenient. Plus, my daughter was so fond of him," the former neighbor recalled.

The woman also knew and liked Alex's girlfriend, Beth Veglahn, a mother of three with whom he shared an apartment upstairs. Beth, a busy mom, worked part-time at night as a custodian for the Lake Elsinore School District and sometimes cleaned houses on the side.

"I was very close to Beth and her kids and nieces," said the woman. "And Alex was always around . . . We often swam together, and Alex was very playful with the kids. He was patient and affectionate and always willing to play games with them."

Around the same time, other locals reported frequently seeing Alex and his young charges at the local McDonald's where his sister worked. He bought them Happy Meals and seemed content spending his free time with other people's children, especially little girls. Still, one McDonald's employee would later recount, it seemed odd. "He was really weird. He was, like, twenty-five at the time, playing with little kids. There's something wrong with that."

But to his former neighbor, nothing seemed amiss. So even after the woman moved away, Avila was a welcome visitor in her home for a year or so, before they fell out of touch.

Then, in late December 1999, came a shocking phone call from her friend Beth Veglahn, who had split from Avila the previous spring.

She heard the chilling words on the other end of the line, but they didn't seem real. Alex Avila, Beth told her, had just been accused of sexually molesting her daughter, Jane, and her niece, Mary, while he baby-sat for the girls earlier that year. Both girls were nine when they reported the abuse in December.

The former neighbor was stunned by the news. Alex had seemed so normal, so harmless. But Beth was a good, trusted friend, and her daughter and niece had always liked Alex — why would they accuse him of something so vile unless it was true?

The woman's heart raced with the grim recollection that Alex had baby-sat for her daughter, too. If he'd molested those girls, what about her baby? Veglahn, still coming to grips with her daughter's and niece's recent disclosures of molestation, was badly shaken herself and couldn't do much to ease her friend's mind. For those who knew Beth and Alex, a dark cloud hung over the usually festive holiday celebrations that year.

Just over a year later, in January 2001, that menacing cloud would return when Alex Avila, his black hair slicked straight back from his distinctive low hairline, cockily strode out of Riverside Superior Court a free man — acquitted of all charges.

After the verdict, Avila quietly disappeared from town. For months to come, customers grabbing coffee or a loaf of bread in the local minimart would gossip that he'd moved away to Anza, California. "Good riddance," was the common sentiment. Lake Elsinore could do without his kind.

But later that year, some strange things happened, according to Beth Veglahn's foster brother Lewis Davis, who had helped her pack her things and move out when she left Avila in March 1999. "One time, Beth's VW van, which was parked on the street, was vandalized. One night a rock crashed through my window. Then someone put sugar in my gas tank, and I found broken eggs in my car," said Davis. It was enough to make them wonder . . . who might have it in for them? "We thought it might be him, but we had no proof."

Then the following fall, Davis recalled, in November 2001, while driving a friend home, he stopped by the local minimart for coffee, and as he was walking in, Alex Avila was walking out.

Davis, the uncle of both girls Avila had been accused of molesting, couldn't resist an opportunity to vent his feelings. "Hey, it's the child molester!" Davis yelled as he came face-to-face with his sister's ex-boyfriend.

"I was proven innocent of that," Avila replied.

Davis and Avila went their separate ways, but Davis was left fuming at the way Avila seemed to have twisted his acquittal. He may have been found "not guilty" of the crimes under the narrow confines of the law, but "proven innocent"? Even though, in his own statement to police, Avila had admitted to "soaping" the bare genitals of one of his victims at least twelve times, he somehow thought he had been "proven innocent"? Davis was stunned by the arrogance.

Despite his self-proclaimed innocence, on July 15, 2002, Avila would drive to the very condo complex in Stanton, California, where his former alleged victim, Jane, had lived with her father, Jim Coker. Avila, who had been cut off from the Veglahns since the trial, may not have known that Coker and his family had moved away some months earlier.

In their hearts, siblings Beth Veglahn, Rosemary Drabek, and Lewis Davis all hold the chilling belief that when Avila drove to the Smoketree Condominiums on that fateful July day, his mission was to find Jane. Instead, perhaps motivated by rage at finding that Jane and her family no longer lived there, he spotted angelic Samantha Runnion playing outside with a friend.

Avila carried the girl kicking and screaming into his car, then sexually assaulted, beat, and smothered her, leaving her naked body in a grotesque spread-eagled pose in a remote spot ten miles from his home in Lake Elsinore.

"He should have been in prison and that little girl would still be alive," said Davis. "My niece [Jane] is pretty upset. She knew little Samantha from the neighborhood in Stanton. She is taking it very hard."

CHAPTER 25

In his open displays of affection for children, Alejandro Avila had created the perfect cover for the child molester who lurked within. Orange County Sheriff Mike Carona has said he is "one hundred percent sure" Avila viciously killed Samantha, a child so cute her face would melt a glacier. If that proves true, then Avila hid enormous rage beneath his mild-mannered exterior, and did it well.

In the days after Avila's arrest for Samantha's murder, his mother, Adelina, and younger sister Elvira, age twenty-two, spoke to reporters from *The Orange County Register* about him. " 'I didn't do it,' " his mother quoted him as saying, " 'and you know God knows I didn't do it, even if I am accused.' "

Once again, in his mind, he was innocent.

The mother and sister supplied little information about his upbringing and claimed they'd never seen Alex's dark side. "He's just a clown. He's just funny," said Elvira.

Adelina, with whom Avila lived at the time of Samantha's murder, told ABC-TV's *Good Morning*

America that before her son's arrest, they had watched news reports of Samantha's disappearance together. "I said they should get that person and tie him up alive and burn him," the mom recalled. "And then Alex said, 'What about the electric chair?' I said, 'No, because he is not going to suffer that much.' "

Adelina's denial was slowly washed away with her son's arrest in the rape and murder of Samantha Runnion. She then admitted to *The Orange County Register* that she recalled having found pornographic images on her son's computer screen. During his earlier molestation trial she had staunchly defended him, testifying on his behalf. Now his last defender, his own mother, was deeply shaken by the brutal crime.

"I hope if he did it God will forgive him," said Adelina.

Alejandro Avila, born March 13, 1975, was the third of six children born to Adelina and her husband, Rafael Rodriges Avila, a Mexican immigrant who held a "green card," which allowed him to live and work legally within the U.S. The family resided in Los Angeles for a time but moved to rural Lake Elsinore in 1989, when Alex was fourteen. Rafael, as he had done in L.A., worked as a butcher.

There, some neighbors remembered Alex as a bit of a "sissy." Alex shied away from rough play with boys, preferring to hang out with girls, said a former neighbor. "His brothers used to tease him about it. They called him 'fairy' and 'fag' and stuff like that."

Often, Alex was seen in public holding the hand of his mother or sister, which did little to bolster his image in his tough brothers' eyes.

Lewis Davis said Avila's brothers, Juan and Ralph, were "gang members" who always courted trouble. In 2001,

Juan was found dead in Rosarito, Mexico, with a bullet in the back of his neck. According to news reports, the shooting was most likely linked to his gang activity.

In the early 1990s, the Avilas began feuding with their neighbor in Lake Elsinore, Kenneth E. Whitney, a married engineer in his thirties, and father of two girls. The Avilas claimed the animosity was racially motivated, that Whitney hated them because they were of Mexican descent. But others suggest that the bad behavior of the Avila boys, Juan and Ralph, caused the feud to escalate. By early 1992, it reached a fatal breaking point.

On February 9 of that year, one of the Avila boys hurled a rock through the window of Whitney's truck. Whitney, then thirty-six, called police and apparently became upset when cops did not arrest the youth. Outraged that the deed would go unpunished, Whitney grabbed and shook the Avila boy he believed was responsible. Cops pulled Whitney away and urged him to calm down.

The incident, however, did not end there, according to court records and a report in *The Riverside Press-Enterprise* newspaper. The next morning, a still-seething Whitney stood in his driveway on Buchanan Street taking pictures of the damage to his truck. When he saw Rafael Avila come outside, he egged him on to settle the dispute "like a man."

Rafael Avila pulled out a .357 Magnum handgun, one similar to the weapon Clint Eastwood's "Dirty Harry" character used in the movies, and blasted Whitney in the chest three times. The neighbor was dead before he hit the pavement.

Rafael Avila, then forty-eight, was charged with murder and carted off to the Robert Presley Detention Center, more commonly known as the Riverside County Jail. Court papers hint that it may not have been Rafael's first brush with the law. In a motion filed on September 16, 1992, seeking to delay the trial, Rafael's lawyer, deputy public defender Forest Wright, said he needed more time to "review additional police reports of incidents outside of Riverside County. Said incidents, whether or not resulting in arrest, are relevant as to purported acts of violence by the defendant."

Wright also asked and received the judge's permission to have Rafael undergo a battery of tests and an examination by a court-appointed psychiatrist, but such reports are sealed to protect the defendant's doctor/patient confidentiality.

Later that year, on December 2, 1992, just eight days before his forty-ninth birthday, Rafael Avila pleaded guilty to the lesser charge of voluntary manslaughter in exchange for a lighter sentence than the twenty-five-years-to-life that a murder conviction would have brought. Five members of Rafael's family were on hand in Department 51 of Riverside Superior Court when he entered his guilty plea, but court records don't say which ones, so it is unclear whether Alex, then seventeen, was among those who came to bid Rafael good-bye.

At the start of the proceeding, Rafael told the judge he had been promised a chance "to speak privately with my family, an hour or two" before going away to prison.

His lawyer begged the judge to allow the sheriff's deputies to remove the manacles that chained Rafael's hands to his waist so he could have some final hugs.

"Mr. Avila wishes to be able to embrace his daughters," said the lawyer. "Just briefly, prior to being transported, and he would respectfully ask the court to allow him some freedom to do that."

Saying it was against policy to remove the defendant's chains, a bailiff balked at the request.

"He can embrace them," ruled Judge Thompson

Hanks. "But I am not going to go contrary to the sheriff's policy on the restraints."

"I don't want to embrace them with the chains," argued Rafael, before asking, "Can you ask my family if they will accept [the chains]?"

The family did not object.

When it came time for Rafael to agree to the basic facts of his crime, a necessary part of the plea process, his stubborn pride showed through again. Right up to the end, Rafael continued to insist that Whitney was armed with a gun when he shot him, although witnesses and cops said no weapon was ever found on or near the victim.

"But is it true that you understand that no weapon was actually found by any of the other witnesses?" Rafael's lawyer asked his client in the presence of the judge.

"At the moment of the shooting," Rafael replied, "he had one in his hand."

Finally, after several such exchanges, Rafael conceded that he understood the police investigation found no weapon on or near the victim. Rafael, it seemed, wanted to believe he was justified in the killing, not really guilty — a mind-set eerily similar to that which his son Alex would display years later, when he boasted he'd been "proven innocent" of the molestation charges.

With his guilty plea complete, Rafael would make one more crack at getting free of his chains for the family embrace.

"Here is another question . . ." Rafael began.

". . . He wants to know if he can release one arm?" the attorney finished the sentence.

Worn down by Rafael's persistence, Judge Hanks replied from his elevated perch on the bench: "We will release one of his arms to embrace his family. We will do this one person at a time; in other words, folks, we can't have you all crowd up at one time."

With that small victory, Rafael began a sixteen-year prison term. After serving just eight years, he won early parole on December 7, 2000 — just three weeks before his son's molestation trial would begin in the same Riverside courthouse where Rafael had pled guilty to taking a life. Not long after, Rafael jumped parole and fled to Mexico, according to news reports, where he allegedly still remains today.

CHAPTER 26

With his father in prison and his troublesome brothers living on the edge of the law, it fell to Alex to become the man of the family. His mother, Adelina, who worked as a bilingual aide in the Lake Elsinore School District, and his younger sisters, Elvira and Adelita, relished having the good-natured Alex around in those grim days after Rafael went away to do his time.

Things were tough financially without Rafael's income, and any extra money Alex could earn was more than welcome. Alex, however, seemed less than motivated in the workplace. Despite his supposed affability and helpfulness, he developed a spotty work history, marked by firings from at least two jobs. In the small town of Lake Elsinore, there are few secrets — word soon spread that Alex had sticky fingers and liked to pilfer from his employers.

"He stole from every place he ever worked," said Lewis Davis. "When he worked at the AM/PM minimart, he ripped off $8,000 from the register, and the owner couldn't pay his fuel bill because of it. He had to go out of business.

"When Alex worked at Wal-Mart as a security guard, he took merchandise, tools, knives, things like that. We know he got fired for stealing, but he told us he was fired for driving the security cart wrecklessly. Alex thought he could talk his way out of anything."

At the time of his arrest for molesting Jane and Mary in January 2000, Alex was working as a delivery driver for Professional Hospital Supply. The company warehoused and distributed medical products, including adult diapers, needles, syringes, bedpans, oxygen masks, and flexible plastic intravenous tubing, which is used to carry IV fluid from its container to the needle inserted in a patient's vein.

At his trial, it was suggested that Avila pilfered some of this plastic tubing, cut it into short sections, and used it to violate Jane, inserting the tubing into her vagina. His own boss at PHS, Jerry Constable, testified that Avila had access to boxes of the type of plastic tubing Jane described in her allegations.

"He was carrying them in his van, and they are sitting in the open warehouse," Constable testified. The notion of Alex pilfering items from his job came as no surprise to Beth Veglahn and Lewis Davis, but the familiar story now took on an added and ugly turn.

But, as Davis saw it, stealing was just one of Alex Avila's many odd personal quirks — Veglahn had told him some other strange things about Alex.

"Even though they lived together for almost three years, she never saw him naked," said Davis. "All the lights had to be off before he would undress. He showered with his underwear on. And he would never expose his feet. He wore socks to bed. My sister talked about it many times, how odd it was."

By the pool, he was often seen wearing rubber water booties, but neighbors thought he wore them to avoid slipping. Beth Veglahn knew otherwise.

And, it appears, his romance with Beth, a woman eleven years his senior, may have been plagued by sexual problems. Their relationship hit the skids at one point in 1998, and Beth moved into her own place for a four-month period. During his child molestation trial, she was asked to explain why they split.

"We didn't have sex," she replied curtly before Avila's defense lawyer, John Pozza, quickly dropped the subject.

When Beth had met Avila in July 1996, he was living with his mother, whom Beth considered a bit overbearing and too controlling of her son. Alex also had his frustrations with Adelina, and it was after a serious fight with his mom that he first decided to move in with Beth in September of that year.

"I forgot what the fight was about," Beth later testified.

Then, on August 31, 1998, trouble came knocking at Beth and Alex's door. Adelina was short of cash and needed a place to live.

"I couldn't afford my apartment that I had," Adelina said. "So I had to put everything in storage. I told Alex my situation, and he says, 'Well you can move in with me.' "

She and her youngest daughter, Adelita, joined Beth and Alex in the cramped one-bedroom apartment. On weekends, Beth's three children would also visit, leaving little room to breathe. Alex's mother and sister stayed until November, putting further strains on the couple's troubled relationship.

Privately, Beth referred to Adelina, now fifty, as "the witch," Davis recalled. "She didn't care for her, to put it mildly."

The relationship between Avila and Beth ended for good

in March 1999. Davis claimed that Beth had become fed up with Avila, who sometimes acted like a man and other times seemed to have the mind of a child. He added that his sister became interested in another man.

"She was talking to this other guy a lot, and Alex was getting basically very weird and possessive," explained Davis. "He started getting angry and violent. He threw a telephone at her. One night she called me and said, 'Lewis, I have to get away from him.' I helped her move her things out at night. And after she left him, he stalked her. I used to have to go to where she worked at night to make sure she got home safely."

During the breakup, Beth never once mentioned any suspicion that Avila had molested her daughter and niece to her brother, who said, "She had no idea. No one did. We had no hint that he liked little girls."

By the time Jane eventually told her mother of the molestation nine months later, Avila had moved on and developed a close friendship with another working mother, who also had a prepubescent daughter. Avila met Annette Hedgepeth around mid-1999 at Professional Hospital Supply, where she also worked as a delivery driver. The two hit it off, and although Annette was married, she regularly socialized with Alex outside work.

Annette visited Avila's home several times "looking at puppies," she testified at his molestation trial. On at least one occasion, she and Avila even took her daughter, Sharlane, age eleven, to Chuck E. Cheese and the movies. Oddly, Annette's son, Phillip, age six, didn't go on the outing but stayed home with his dad. Hedgepeth insisted she and Avila were "just friends" and said her husband was aware of their relationship.

Hedgepeth, who earned $9.05 an hour at her job, proved to be a very loyal friend, using some of her own money and borrowing more from her mother to scrape together the $2,500 down payment for Avila's bail in January 2000, when he was arrested on the molestation charges. Later, when he was arrested a second time in February 2000 for allegedly threatening Rosemary Drabek, she bailed him out again, this time selling her truck for $2,000 to help raise the money.

From the witness stand, Hedgepeth made it clear she thought Avila had been falsely accused. Although she had a daughter of her own to think about, she was willing to bail him out.

She declared of the charge, "I don't believe it."

Once again, Avila had worked his magic of deceit. Annette Hedgepeth didn't believe the Alex she knew, who raised puppies and patiently played kids' games at Chuck E. Cheese, was a child molester. Had Alex not been arrested for molesting Beth's daughter and niece, would he have found a way, over time, to make Annette's daughter Sharlane, his next victim? Had that been his plan?

In the aftermath of Samantha Runnion's murder, one of Avila's former neighbors from Lake Elsinore, a woman who had given him the run of her apartment and left her three-year-old daughter in his care, has had some sleepless nights.

Thinking back, she realized she had been duped.

"Little did I know that I allowed a monster into my life and into the life of my baby girl!" the woman said, scared to even reveal her name. "Now my head is constantly swirling with all the unthinkable acts that might have gone on between Alex and my daughter. This is a nightmare I will have to live with for the rest of my life."

Avila, she said, taught her a harsh lesson — sexual predators don't come with signs around their necks.

"Don't be fooled by men who seem nice. Alex was fun, gentle. He never drank and he seemed great with kids. I now know that you can never tell when someone's a sex offender."

And for Lewis Davis, uncle of both girls Avila was acquitted of molesting, the painful saga has left him with just one hope: that this time around, for little Samantha Runnion, justice will be done.

Noting news reports that the Orange County district attorney has a strong case against Avila, Davis cautiously said, "There was good evidence in my nieces' case, too. I didn't think he was going to get away with it last time, either."

An Angel Vanishes

CHAPTER 27

While the murders of Ashley Pond and Miranda Gaddis, Danielle van Dam, and Samantha Runnion are immeasurably horrible and tragic, there is the small consolation that the evil men believed responsible for these acts, Ward F. Weaver III, David Alan Westerfield, and Alejandro Avila, have been caught. These predators either have been, or will be, dealt with in the criminal justice system.

There can, at least, be closure for the victims' families in reclaiming their children's bodies for dignified burial, and in beginning the painful process of accepting their violent deaths at the hands of perpetrators who are now behind bars.

For Edward and Lois Smart, however, there is no glimmer of consolation or closure. The parents of fourteen-year-old Elizabeth Smart, who was snatched from her bed in her family's $1.19 million Salt Lake

City, Utah, home in the early morning hours of June 5, 2002, are left to cope with more questions than answers.

Samantha Runnion's case illustrates that a crime can be solved quickly when eyewitnesses, police, and a vigilant public all join forces to catch the perpetrator and when police response is immediate and blunder-free. Elizabeth's still-unsolved abduction, on the other hand, shows how delays in reporting a disappearance and a sluggish investigation can have disastrous results.

The first days of June had been exhausting and emotionally draining ones for Ed, a forty-seven-year-old mortgage and real estate broker, Lois, forty-five, a homemaker, and their six children. Lois's father, Myron L. Francom, eighty-one, had died on May 29 after a month-long illness, during which Lois and her children had spent every spare minute by his bedside. Francom, the father of eight and a pillar of the Mormon Church, died in his own bed, at home, surrounded by loving family.

On June 2, a funeral was held at the East Millcreek 15th Ward building, the local Mormon Church, attended by nearly two hundred people. Lovely Elizabeth, a willowy blond who stood five feet six inches tall and weighed just 105 pounds, played her harp at the solemn service, and many mourners marveled at her poise and talent.

A reception with food and soft drinks (Mormons are forbidden to drink alcoholic beverages or coffee) followed at the church's Ward Hall and stretched into the late afternoon. In their tight-knit Mormon community, the Francoms and the Smarts (Lois was one of eight children; Ed, one of six) had a huge extended family and many friends who turned out to offer condolences. Lois and Ed would graciously receive many a compliment on how Elizabeth was growing into a fine young woman and an accomplished harpist, a musical skill prized in the Mormon community.

Although the funeral had been tiring, Elizabeth returned to Bryant Intermediate School the next day, Tuesday, June 4, where she was completing the eighth grade. That afternoon, Elizabeth, an avid runner who hoped to make the high school track team the next year, went for a jog in the neighborhood, her buttercup-blond ponytail swinging from side to side behind her. Elizabeth's little sister, Mary Katherine, age nine, tagged along by her side.

Later that evening, the entire Smart family attended an awards ceremony at Elizabeth's school. On their way out, Ed left the garage door open, apparently thinking it was safe for the few hours they would be gone. At the joyful ceremony, Elizabeth received citations for fitness and academics. It would be the last time Elizabeth's teachers and schoolmates would ever see her.

Upon returning home, the sleepy Smart sisters retired upstairs to their pink and off-white bedroom, where they shared a queen-size antique-style poster bed. One of seven bedrooms in the sprawling Smart home, the girls' room was decidedly feminine, with a border of pink flowers and green leaves stenciled along the upper portion of the cream-colored walls and a frilly dust ruffle on the bed. Dolls and stuffed animals lined the shelves.

Ed and Lois, exhausted from the trying week, and Elizabeth's three younger brothers, also went to bed, leaving the oldest brother Charles, sixteen, the last one up. Studying for his exams at East High School, Charles stayed up until 11 p.m., but heard nothing unusual.

What happened next, and precisely when it happened, has never been fully clarified, but sometime around 1 a.m., a man, reportedly armed with a gun, quietly entered the girls' bedroom without waking Ed and Lois, who slept in a bedroom across the hall, just to the right of the upstairs landing.

What is known about how Elizabeth was taken comes from Mary Katherine, who was awakened from her slumber as the gunman ordered Elizabeth from the bed in the dark room.

According to initial police reports of the crime, the gunman directly threatened Mary Katherine that if she told anyone or made any noise her sister would be harmed. So after the intruder left with Elizabeth, the angelic golden-haired child, who looked like a miniature version of her lanky older sister, remained frozen and silent in her bed for two hours before deciding to alert her parents.

The gunman allowed Elizabeth, who was wearing only red silk Chinese-style pajamas, to grab a pair of white canvas Polo shoes before taking her away from her home on Kristianna Circle.

When terrified Mary Katherine finally went to her parents' room, perhaps about 3 a.m., she told her father, "A man took Elizabeth."

At first, "I thought she was having a bad dream," Ed later told reporters.

But soon he and his wife were scouring the home, realizing Elizabeth was, indeed, gone. Considering that most kidnap victims who are murdered are killed within three hours of the time of abduction, two precious hours had already been lost by Mary Katherine's understandable delay in telling her parents. But what happened next would make things worse.

Instead of calling police immediately, Ed and Lois began their own search of the sprawling 6,600-square-foot home and grounds. They called church leaders and relatives on the phone and even went across the street to alert their neighbor, wealthy executive H. Brent Beesley, whose own daughter had been the target of a foiled kidnap-for-ransom plot a decade earlier.

Elizabeth's brother Charles said his parents woke him at 4 a.m. and told him she was missing. "We just started yelling for her . . . My mom walked down [into the kitchen] and noticed the screen was cut and she just screamed," Charles told the *Deseret News*, the local Mormon-owned paper. Ed Smart finally called police at 4:01 a.m., according to the Salt Lake City Police Department's dispatch log. Driving at a rate of sixty miles per hour on Utah's open roads in the dead of night, the kidnapper could easily have been 180 miles away by then.

And when cops arrived, they found at least a half dozen neighbors, in addition to Ed and Lois and their five other children, milling about the house and yard, by their very presence contaminating the crime scene with extraneous footprints, clothing fibers, hair and fingerprints. The cops had an uphill battle from the start.

The initial police bulletin, based on Mary Katherine's description, said the gunman was white, about twenty-eight to forty years old, with black hair, medium build, wearing a white baseball cap without lettering, tan pants, and a tan or white jacket. But oddly, when reporters asked if a composite sketch of the kidnapper would be forthcoming, cops quietly said they didn't think the child had gotten a good enough look to assist a police artist in creating a sketch.

But, reporters wondered, if she'd seen enough to know his hair color, even though he was wearing a cap, and his approximate age, hadn't she seen at least part of his face? Wouldn't it be worth a try? That question bugged no one more than Marc Klaas, the father of kidnapped and murdered twelve-year-old Polly Klaas, who, in the wake of his daughter's death, became a nationally known child protection advocate. Klaas was on the scene in Salt Lake to provide expert commentary for a television network.

From the beginning, Klaas was clamoring to bring in Jeannie Boylan, a famous sketch artist (her drawing of the 1990s Unabomber suspect was seen by millions) with expertise in questioning and drawing out crucial information from terrified witnesses, especially children.

But when Klaas approached Tom Smart, Ed's older brother and the family's appointed "official spokesman," with the suggestion, he was turned down flat.

Klaas had heard that Ed Smart favored the idea of calling in Boylan, so he couldn't understand Tom Smart's resistance in the face of such a desperate situation. Elizabeth had now been missing six days, despite the tireless efforts of thousands of volunteers who were organized and trained by the Texas-based Laura Recovery Center. The volunteers had combed miles of the Utah landscape, some on foot, some on all-terrain vehicles, and others in airplanes and helicopters, to no avail.

On June 11 and 12, Klaas, speaking on FOX News Channel's popular *O'Reilly Factor* program, blasted the missing girl's uncle for hindering the investigation and openly questioned his motivations.

Also by that time, news reports had surfaced that Ed Smart had submitted to a police lie-detector test. Then, on the night of June 12, Tom Smart disclosed on CNN's *Larry King Live* that he, too, had taken a polygraph test at the request of police, but he did not discuss the results.

"Everybody is suspect on this," he said.

In the coming days, TV and newspaper reports would quote anonymous sources saying that Ed had passed his test, but Tom's was "inconclusive." Officially, police wouldn't comment on either man's test result.

Tom Smart also raised some eyebrows with other remarks he made during the *Larry King* show, which was guest-hosted that night by veteran prosecutor Nancy Grace. When she asked him to deliver a message to the kidnapper in case he was watching, Tom Smart's reply was bizarre, at best.

"I believe that this person is not a bad person at all. And our family has felt this strongly for a while. And there's been a comfort here for a while. This is just somebody who actually likes Elizabeth. We don't know. We have issues. We have been ripped apart by our polygraph. I don't know who has done what with my brothers . . .

"And we pray that whoever this is will know that the family is full of compassion towards everybody because this is a wonderful story in a lot of ways. Because it's about, foremost, a beautiful, little, angelic girl . . . It crosses the boundaries on everything. It's an amazing story."

CHAPTER 28

On June 13, 2002, *The Salt Lake Tribune*, which unlike Salt Lake's other local paper, the *Deseret News*, is not owned by Mormons, took a bold stance. The shocking front-page report, citing four unnamed law enforcement sources, said some evidence at the scene suggested the kidnapping might have been an "inside job." It appeared the kitchen window screen, believed to have been the kidnapper's point of entry, may have been cut by someone *inside* the home, not outside, to stage the appearance of a break-in.

Soon reports on MSNBC and other outlets went farther down this road, reporting that police sources said they didn't think a man could have entered the home through the tall, narrow window, which operated on a crank. There were no snagged clothing fibers on the cut screen, as one would expect if someone had crawled through the narrow opening.

And, while the window was nearly six feet above ground, there were no scuff marks on the outside of the home, which would be expected if someone had climbed or shimmied up to get in. The home had no other signs of forced entry.

It appeared police were closely eyeing family members and acquaintances as possible suspects in the case, a normal step in most kidnapping investigations but one that took on a more sinister tone in light of Tom Smart's strange behavior and the troubling kitchen window evidence.

Ed Smart acknowledged early on that he had failed to set the home's burglar alarm system before going to bed that night. "I grew up in this neighborhood. I was never one for locking doors and windows," he told the *Deseret News* on June 9. Yet, in a seeming contradiction of his philosophy, he also told the newspaper he had "locked all the doors on the basement and main floors" that night before retiring.

More than a week later, at a press briefing on June 17, Ed Smart told reporters about how he had left the garage door open while the family attended Elizabeth's school awards ceremony the evening of the kidnapping. He said he shut the garage door before going to bed, but this revelation raised the possibility that an intruder could have entered the home earlier and hidden inside until the family fell asleep.

There are also questions about the timeliness and quality of interviews police conducted with the key witness in the case, Mary Katherine Smart. It is unclear whether Ed and Lois may have initially shielded Mary Katherine from direct police interviews in an effort to protect the traumatized child, or whether detectives simply failed to inform their chief and other department spokesmen about what the girl had said.

But on June 18, Chief Rick Dinse told the media that his earlier report of Mary Katherine's account, which claimed the kidnapper had directly threatened her, was incorrect and had been "based on secondhand accounts."

Now, he said, Mary Katherine had merely heard the kidnapper threaten Elizabeth; the suspect had never spoken to the younger sister because she was pretending to be asleep. The real reason for her two-hour delay in telling her parents was because when she first attempted to go tell them, she had peeked out her bedroom door and seen the kidnapper still in the house. So she went back into bed and remained there about two hours before finally getting the nerve to venture out again. One hoped the detectives working the case were better informed than their chief appeared to have been.

Police would not reveal specifics on who questioned the child and when, but they steadfastly maintained that Mary Katherine's story had been consistent from the beginning. "She hasn't wavered one bit from her original statement," Dinse said.

The chief also clarified the child's description of the killer, saying he had worn a light-colored short-billed golf cap, not a baseball cap, as initially reported. And, he added, the suspect had dark hair on his hands and forearms. Still, without a sketch of the kidnapper's face, a tool that would prove so helpful in solving Samantha Runnion's kidnapping a month later, these new details would not do much to identify the gunman who had taken Elizabeth. It was too little, too late.

Eleven days had passed since Elizabeth's kidnapping, and while there had been many tips that didn't pan out, not one credible sighting of the girl or her abductor had been phoned in to the nationally broadcast Salt Lake City Police hotline number. The National Center for Missing and Exploited Children also immediately posted Elizabeth's photo and description, as well as the kidnapper's, at the top of its popular website. Still, despite the agency's plea, no one called its 1-800-THE-LOST number with any useful information.

Officials were left to explore traditional suspects in any missing persons case — direct relatives. Elizabeth Smart, though, had twenty-nine aunts and uncles and more than seventy cousins. By late June, when the investigation had unearthed no family bombshells, a frustrated police insider confided to *Newsweek*, "We need a break in this case."

To their credit, police had doggedly pursued a few early leads, but many came up cold. One was that of Bret Michael Edmunds, a twenty-six-year-old homeless probation violator with a minor rap sheet, whose car a milkman had seen in the Smart's neighborhood two days before the kidnapping.

A nationwide manhunt for Edmunds was launched on June 12. After several false sightings in Utah, Texas, and elsewhere, Edmunds was finally caught in Martinsburg, West Virginia. On June 21, a suspicious nurse at the hospital where he showed up with a drug overdose turned him in to the FBI.

Salt Lake detectives on Smart's case flew across the country to question Edmunds in his hospital bed, but he was soon cleared. Among other factors, Edmunds, it turned out, was a hulking guy, six foot two, and notably obese, weighing nearly 250 pounds. Mary Katherine had described the kidnapper as five eight to five ten with a "medium build."

Another roller-coaster ride for the Smarts and investigators on the case had screeched to a halt.

On June 24, police announced they had new suspect — ex-convict and former handyman at the Smart home, Richard Albert Ricci. Ricci, whose twenty-nine-year criminal record included robbery and other felony convictions, had been questioned by cops the day after Elizabeth's disappearance. He was subsequently arrested on an unrelated parole violation on June 14.

Once in custody, cops questioned him again, but Ricci was vague about his actions and whereabouts between May 31 and June 8, Dinse said, adding, "Mr. Ricci denies involvement."

Ricci had done odd jobs and carpentry during a remodeling project in the Smarts' home the previous year, but he and some other workers were fired when Lois Smart noticed items, including jewelry, missing from the home. Lois's instincts were right. During a search of Ricci's mobile home in June 2002, cops found $3,500 worth of items taken from the Smart home a year earlier, including jewelry, a perfume bottle, and a wine glass filled with seashells.

On July 11, Ricci was charged with burglary and theft in connection with the June 2001 incident. He'd apparently broken into the Smarts' home to steal at least once before, but did he take Elizabeth?

Ed Smart said he never would have hired Ricci if he'd known of his criminal history, but he conceded Ricci had "seemed nice enough" at the time. In fact, Ed had given Ricci his old 1990 white Jeep Cherokee and allowed him to pay for the vehicle with his labors.

That very Jeep Cherokee soon became the focal point of growing suspicion that Ricci might be involved in Elizabeth's disappearance.

Auto mechanic Neth Moul, who runs a repair shop near Ricci's home, said the suspect picked the Jeep up from his shop on May 30 and returned it on June 8, caked in mud and with five hundred to a thousand additional miles on the odometer.

Moul says he saw Ricci stuff the Jeep's two front seat covers into a black plastic garbage bag, which he then slung over a posthole digger (a double-handled shovel-like tool used to dig holes for fence posts) that he had removed from the vehicle. Moul, who has told his story under oath to a federal grand jury probing Elizabeth's disappearance, said Ricci took the items and walked across the street, where a man was waiting to drive him away.

Cops said Ricci never gave a believable explanation for the hundreds of extra miles put on his Jeep in early June, but his lawyer claimed the car was still in the repair shop when Elizabeth disappeared, disputing Moul's account.

Other witnesses also described odd behavior by Ricci. His neighbor Andy Thurber said he awoke the morning of Elizabeth's disappearance and encountered Ricci outside. "He had dug a hole underneath my porch," Thurber told reporters. "I thought it was really strange." Eventually, it was discovered that nothing had been placed into that hole.

Ricci's wife, Angela, insisted that he was home in be with her at the time Elizabeth was abducted. She told cops he went to bed at 10:30 p.m. and that she joined him in the same bed between 1 and 2 a.m. "He was there when I went to bed and there when I got up at 6 a.m.," she said.

But friends and neighbors of the Riccis, including Carma Tolman, said Angela did not seem so sure of her husband's whereabouts. "Angela went around the neighborhood asking people if they had seen him leave late at night," Tolman said.

And Angela's longtime friend Deann Newhouse, a forty-five-year-old housekeeper, shattered the wife's story, claiming Angela had confided in her about her own doubts. "I had asked Angela a million times since Elizabeth went missing if she was sure she knew where Rick was on the night of the kidnapping. Each time she said he was with her in bed." But in a tearful admission around June 17, Newhouse said that Angela blurted out, "To tell you the truth, I honestly don't know where Rick was that night."

Newhouse, who also testified under oath before the grand jury, said Angela Ricci revealed that although Rick had gone to bed around 10 p.m., she took sleeping pills and fell asleep on the couch watching TV and never got into bed, so she couldn't be sure if her husband remained in the house all night. Newhouse said Angela confessed: "I was out like a log."

A spokesman for Ricci's lawyer, David K. Smith, denied Angela used sleeping pills that night and said Angela stood by her statement to cops that her husband was in bed with her on the night of the abduction.

In late June, FBI agents working the case searched the home of Ricci's father-in-law, Dave Morse Sr., age sixty-eight, who lived in the trailer next door to Ricci's. They seized two golf caps, including a light-colored one like the kidnapper wore, and a machete from his toolshed. But, Morse told *USA Today*, Ricci never borrowed the golf caps and did not have a key to the locked toolshed. "I think they are grasping at straws. There's always a chance, but I don't think he did it," Morse opined.

The questions about Ricci's alibi and the extra miles on his Jeep were tantalizing circumstantial evidence. But there was one glaring problem: Ricci had worked in the Smart home for months during 2001 and was well-known to Mary Katherine. If he was the kidnapper, wouldn't she have recognized him or his voice? Cops did not have an answer, except to say that she did not get a good look at the intruder's face, the same reason they had given for not attempting to produce a sketch of the kidnapper.

Some experts wonder whether Mary Katherine may have unintentionally buried some memories of the incident as a means of "self-protection" because they were too traumatic to hold in her conscious mind.

"She may have suppressed some details of this terrible crime," said Wendy Murphy, a former prosecutor in Boston, Massachusetts, and noted child advocate. "She may be psychologically incapable of remembering important facts. It requires very careful, experienced questioning to reveal everything without causing further trauma to the child."

But Murphy holds out hope that a key memory could resurface at some point. "You never know what could spark a memory. Seeing someone on TV who looks like the gunman, hearing her sister's name, smelling an aftershave. It could all come flooding out in one burst, or drip out, bit by bit."

Cops still had yet to find a shred of physical evidence linking Ricci to Elizabeth's disappearance when, on August 27, 2002, Ricci collapsed in his jail cell, stricken by a blood clot in his brain. He underwent emergency surgery but never regained consciousness. He died three days later when his wife gave the okay to remove life supports. Any secrets he may have known went with him to the grave.

In the aftermath of Ricci's death, Elizabeth's case remains unsolved and open for further investigation. Her parents continue daily prayer sessions and hold out hope that she is still alive.

"Every morning when we get up, we say to ourselves, today is the day we will see her again," said Ed Smart. "We have to believe that — the alternative is too painful to think about."

Investigators are reportedly split in their opinions of what happened to Elizabeth. Some Salt Lake City detectives think Ricci was the culprit, while others, particularly in the ranks of the FBI, think he was simply an easy target in a baffling investigation.

"We'll find Elizabeth with or without Ricci. He's not the only avenue we are pursuing in this case," said a high-ranking federal law enforcement official. "This isn't over."

Inside the Predator's Mind

CHAPTER 29

Child predators can, and do, hide among us. Some, like David Westerfield, masquerade as talented engineers and devoted dads. Others, like Ward F. Weaver III, pose as concerned parent-substitutes or confidants to other people's troubled kids. And then there's Alejandro Avila, who disguised himself as the ever-willing baby-sitter, always eager to help out busy moms or take their kids to McDonald's for Happy Meals.

In the baffling case of Elizabeth Smart, cops don't know who stole the girl from her bed or what has happened to her since, but evidence suggests the perpetrator was someone familiar with the family's sprawling 6,600-square-foot home, someone who knew how to get around inside the darkened house and which of the seven bedrooms Elizabeth slept in. Someone, perhaps, who had been in the home before, who had the family's trust but held a dark secret in his cold heart.

Dr. Charles Bahn is a professor of forensic psychology at John Jay College of Criminal Justice in New York who received his Ph.D. in psychology from Columbia University. In addition to his work as a professor, Bahn also lectures on psychological profiling at the FBI Academy in Virginia and has worked with numerous police and federal agencies and served as a trainer in hostage negotiations.

Bahn believes Westerfield, Weaver, and Avila cover the broad spectrum of child killers. But whatever glimpses they provide into the demented psyche of a predator, they also demonstrate the near futility of attempting to recognize one before he strikes. There is, unfortunately, no precise blueprint of psychological and environmental factors that creates a child killer, no stock reason why they choose young victims, and no set modus operandi for how some carry out their evil plans.

There is no better evidence of how well child killers can blend into the community than David Westerfield. His longtime neighbors on Treeridge Terrace, with whom he had played Trivial Pursuit and Pictionary for years, had no clue. The parents of schoolmates who saw Westerfield cheerfully attending his daughter's and son's swim meets, soccer games, and concerts, had no inkling.

Westerfield's professional colleagues described a bright, dedicated engineer, who designed medical devices to help people — not a sadistic pervert. And even Brenda van Dam, who brought little Danielle to Westerfield's home to sell Girl Scout cookies just days before the murder, clearly had no idea that a killer hid beneath the normal facade.

Cases like Westerfield's, where a seemingly law-abiding perpetrator commits his first serious sex crime/murder in middle age, are not uncommon.

"It's not a totally unfamiliar pattern," explains Bahn. Many such offenders spend years successfully suppressing their desires and fantasies because they are, in fact, disgusted by their own thoughts. They can sometimes hold off for years, in some cases forever, unless or until something significant triggers them to act on their urges.

"All sexual deviance is on a continuum. Westerfield is probably on the lower end of that continuum. The sad thing about it is — and the reason he probably didn't do this earlier in life — is that while it excites him, the whole idea also disgusts him. There is part of himself he hates. So what do we do with things in ourselves that disgust us? We suppress them."

Bahn explains that any number of factors could lead a suppressor to act out late in life as did Westerfield, who was almost fifty when he killed Danielle. For these types, something has to set them off, but what that actually is can vary. It might be viewing hard-core pornography, as Westerfield had in his home, or just walking past a playground.

"It's hard to say what leads to the final breaking point. In some cases it's that they are getting old and they've never done what they always wanted to do. Sometimes they see a stimulus, perhaps a television show that isn't exactly what they had in mind but which stimulates their thinking along that line. Something triggers it."

In Westerfield's case, Bahn believes his choice of Danielle van Dam as his victim may have been spurred by his own heavy drinking at Dad's Café on the night of the kidnapping. In addition, seeing Brenda van Dam out with her girlfriends in the same bar, just a day or so after the mother had brought her cute little daughter into his home to sell cookies, may have also contributed.

"Alcohol often plays a role in these things. We lose some of our inhibitions when we drink, and seeing the mother in the bar might be interpreted by him as 'license.' What this means to him is, she [Brenda] is a bad person, therefore, in his logic, it's not going to be quite as malicious. In his mind, 'They got what's coming to them,' as far as the parents were concerned."

While there is nothing to suggest that Brenda van Dam acted inappropriately in the bar, just her being there may have been, in Westerfield's sick mind, enough to justify his own acts. He was simply a time bomb, looking for an excuse to blow. Anything could have lit that fuse.

Danielle van Dam's body was badly decomposed when found, so the medical examiner had a difficult task in determining exactly what had been done to her before or after death. But, says Bahn, he would not be surprised to find that a perpetrator fitting Westerfield's profile would inflict postmortem, or after-death, injury on his victim.

The profile gets even uglier.

"Let's begin with a psychological variable that is often found with sexual crimes . . . the enormous amount of damage the perpetrator does *after* the crime, the mutilation, essentially, that sometimes occurs . . . It's an attempt at destruction. It's rage against self, an attempt to undo the act by destroying it. And they blame the child for stimulating it." Sick child killers, therefore, even blame the victim after death, and they seek to punish the child with further brutal treatment.

"They blame the victim for being seductive," explains Bahn.

Westerfield's case also provides insight to counter a common misconception: Laymen often mistakenly believe that all child killers are pedophiles — a specific type of adult sexual deviant who prefers to have sex with children.

That is not necessarily the case for all child killers, even when there is a sexual element to the crime, says Bahn. While Westerfield clearly fantasized about sex with little girls, there is no evidence that children were his overall sexual preference. He was married for seventeen years and had adult girlfriends after his divorce from his first wife. Some adults, even those who prefer sex with other adults, may molest children simply out of curiosity, easy availability, or a desire to hurt a loved one of the molested child. These non-pedophile molesters are called situational molesters.

But Alejandro Avila, who is accused of killing Samantha Runnion, does appear to fit the pedophile mold. He sought out children at every opportunity, whether by hanging around the playground and swimming pool at his apartment complex, baby-sitting, or taking neighborhood children on outings to McDonald's. He chose a girlfriend, Beth Veglahn, who had children. And while he was accused of repeatedly sexually molesting her daughter and niece, both about nine at the time of the assaults, Veglahn revealed that he wasn't having sex with her, which created problems in their relationship.

Bahn believes Avila is much closer "to that picture of a complete pedophile" than Westerfield. And, he says, noting Avila's habit of spending all his free time with small children, "One of the ways to be a pedophile is to become a Pied Piper, so you can have a lot of victims available.

"There are people who . . . hang around playgrounds or take a job with the Boy Scouts. Molesters often feel they are doing good for the child they are assaulting. When they are not molesting, they are busy doing things for the child, they entice the child with ice cream and give them candy afterwards. They give the child a lot of attention and think they are going to establish a good, loving relationship."

Avila eventually progressed to a point where his sexual gratification required more than just molesting kids; it became entwined with violence. What Bahn found most noteworthy and chilling about his behavior was the ghastly way he left Samantha's dead body — naked and spread-eagled — and the message that revealed.

"It's a statement, 'This is what I do, this is what I enjoy

doing.' It's also blaming the child, once again, for being a seductress."

Unlike Westerfield, who Bahn believes was disgusted with his own murderous act and tried to "erase" it, the obscene display of Samantha's body shows Avila was not in the least bit ashamed of what he had done. "He is deriving power from it —'Look what I can do and get away with.'

"My hypothesis on this man [Avila] is that he derives sexual satisfaction out of accomplishing a violent assault. On one level, the sex is subordinate to the violence. I think it's very likely that he would have done it again."

Lastly comes Ward Weaver III, the suspected killer of Ashley Pond and Miranda Gaddis, who may be altogether incapable of even grasping the concept of right and wrong. His consistent, violent conduct since childhood, Bahn believes, is indicative of an antisocial personality — a true "psychopath" in common parlance — one who is completely amoral. He has no empathy for the suffering of others and exists simply to satisfy his own desires, whatever they may be, without remorse.

"It isn't that he thinks things he's done are wrong or disgusting. He doesn't have any standard at all. He could as easily eat an orange or chew a kid's ear off. It doesn't matter to him. If that is what he feels like doing, he'll do it. This guy is not even angry at the victims. He's beyond that."

Weaver's personal history is full of examples of the type of conduct Bahn describes. As a boy, he shot his little sister with a BB gun and laughed. Later, when he was in his teens, a female relative reported that he beat and raped her repeatedly over a five-year period and walked away smiling as she cried. At age twenty-three, Weaver, unprovoked, bashed a teenage family friend on the head with a concrete block. In that instance, he later told a probation officer that sometimes he just "blows." Ward beat his first wife, Maria, for years, according to his oldest son, and bashed his second wife, Kristi Sloan, on the head with a frying pan while she slept. The list goes on and on.

"It's all part of a pattern," explains Bahn — such a psychopath destroys everything in his path.

"These people lie, cheat, steal, commit acts of violence, without a second thought. They just satisfy their own instincts and pleasure on an hour-by-hour basis . . . These are people who, when they are children, slice up a live cat to see what the cat's reaction will be, they pull the wings off birds . . . They feel a lack of empathy entirely with other people. 'I'm going to bash her head and see what happens.' If you talk to them, often their motive is curiosity rather than rage or something of that kind."

After the concrete block attack, Weaver admitted to a probation officer he wasn't angry at the victim and she had never done anything to him. He'd just attacked her for no reason, he said, brushing the conduct off as something he was prone to do when drinking or taking drugs, as he had that night.

The pattern with Weaver, according to Bahn, is one of a repeat violent offender.

"If you ask me the probability, I'd say it's ninety percent that he's done it [murder] before . . . But he put less effort into this one. Burying the bodies in the backyard is less effort. He could have been getting complacent."

Keeping the victims' bodies on his property, Bahn says, "is proof to himself that he can get away with it. It goes along with the amoral stance." Weaver probably wanted a reminder of his conquests close by, trophies of sorts.

"Weaver has no guilt. That's why, when reporters came to his house, he could stand up and say 'I'm innocent,' even though the bodies were buried there. For him, it's over. He's looking forward to the next thing. 'Look what I did to the cat, now let's see what I can do with the dog.'"

Although criminal profilers and psychologists like Bahn have studied the lives of many child killers, they have yet to find the formula that creates one. Many child predators are abused as children, but not all. Westerfield's sister reported he had had an idyllic childhood free of abuse, while Weaver's sister said their stepfather severely beat all the children, including Ward. Thus far, Avila's family members have not said if he was abused, although his father did show a violent temper when he fatally shot a neighbor over a minor dispute.

"When someone combines overt violence with sexuality, there's a higher probability they were abused as children, but not always," explains Bahn.

In their book, *Sexual Homicide: Patterns and Motives*, authors Robert Ressler, Ann Burgess, and John Douglas say sex killers are often those who, for a variety of reasons, fail to form strong family or community ties.

"For children growing up, the quality of their attachments to parents and other members of the family is most important to how these children, as adults, relate to and value other members of society." Many sex killers, Ressler et al. wrote, were also found to have experienced "a high degree of instability in home structure," including frequent relocation and "minimal attachment to community."

Westerfield's family moved three times in his youth, but his parents reportedly got along well and provided a stable home wherever they went. Weaver's family life was highly unsettled from the time of his birth, plagued by domestic violence and then divorce. As a youth, he moved often due to his father's instability, his parents' divorce, his mother's remarriage, and other factors. Avila's history is less clear, although his family did move from Los Angeles to small-town Lake Elsinore when he was fourteen. Avila was seventeen by the time his family encountered serious disruption when his father was sent to prison for killing the neighbor, but he remained close to his mother and sisters, keeping what was left of the family intact.

Again, each man walked a different path in life, but all three wound up committing the most despicable of acts. Those seeking a single, clear portrait of the child killer may be left unsettled, Bahn admits.

There are trends, but no rules.

"There isn't a common thread. Different kinds of people, under different kinds of stress, and for different reasons, kill children."

Out of the Ashes

CHAPTER 30

Unfortunately, in the end there are almost too many child abductions and murders to cover. The media inevitably latches on to the stories that strike a chord, either for the sheer brutality of a killer or for their innocent victims. Whether a search is intense and a resolution swift, as with the case of Samantha Runnion, or mistakes are made and finality never reached, as with the abduction of Elizabeth Smart, families are left to cope with tragedy. For all, there will be a certain pain never relieved. For the following cases, however, heartbreak led to new resolve.

On July 27, 1981, Reve Walsh went with her son, Adam, to shop at the Sears store near the family's Hollywood, Florida, home. A few other kids had gathered in front of a video game in the toy department, and the mother left the boy there momentarily while she ventured a few aisles away. When she returned, Adam had vanished. Reve began calling her son's name, approached other shoppers, and then told a security guard. After more than half an hour, the store made an announcement: "Adam Walsh, please come to customer service."

Two weeks later, Reve and her husband, John, were in New York City, appearing on *Good Morning America* and pleading for Adam's return. Later that same day, the Hollywood police called them in their hotel room with the news — two fishermen had found a head bobbing in a canal in Vero Beach, Florida, 120 miles north of Hollywood. The features were so distorted that a family friend was unable to recognize Adam, and eventually dental records had to confirm the identity. While Reve wept, John trashed their hotel room. No arrest in the brutal killing would ever be made.

The aftermath of his son's murder left John Walsh devastated. Among other things Walsh had to endure was a time when authorities caught a serial abductor who had made an audiotape of himself while torturing and murdering his victims. Walsh had to listen to it, trying to determine whether any of the cries sounded familiar. None did, but the voices still echo in his head and would eventually lead to thoughts of suicide. Instead, Walsh decided then and there to bring his personal pain into the public spotlight, and he began a national campaign to help other children.

Reve and John Walsh had initially traveled to Washington, D.C., to ask for assistance from their senator, Paula Hawkins. Upon arrival, they made their way from the airport to Capitol Hill, passing buildings that were dedicated to every cause imaginable.

"Can you take us to the Children's Building?" Reve asked their cabdriver. They learned that there was no such place — no organization that might help them or other families of missing children.

Walsh left a well-paying job as a developer of resort

hotels and went about creating such a system. He testified before congressional committees on behalf of the Missing Children's Act, which would produce funds and a mandate for the creation of a nationwide database of computerized information. The act also ordered that the FBI's National Crime Information Computer be used and that local FBI offices assist parents of missing children. He was a guest of President Reagan in a 1982 Rose Garden ceremony to mark the signing of the bill into law. Two years later, in 1984, Walsh and his wife founded the National Center for Missing and Exploited Children.

Today, the NCMEC exists as a private, nonprofit organization that works in cooperation with the U.S. Department of Justice's Office of Juvenile Justice and Delinquency Prevention. It has become the nation's foremost resource center for child protection, spearheading national efforts to locate and recover missing children and to raise public awareness about ways to prevent abduction, molestation, and sexual exploitation of children. These goals are accomplished by coordinating the efforts of law enforcement, social service agencies, elected officials, judges, prosecutors, and educators, in both the public and private sectors.

Anything that can help is now being utilized. The NCMEC provides a wide range of free services to law enforcement including: technical case assistance; information analysis and dissemination; photograph and poster preparation; age enhancement of photographs; facial reconstruction and imaging; database searches; educational materials; and training. They also maintain a twenty-four-hour multilingual hotline and a website, all intended to assist parents and law enforcement agencies by creating a central location to receive reports of missing children; to provide information on how to better safeguard children; and even to offer reunification assistance to parents in cases where a child is found.

Although today John Walsh is best known for his television show *America's Most Wanted*, the men and women of the organization he helped found, the NCMEC, are still hard at work. To date, through their various programs, the NCMEC has helped locate more than fifty thousand missing children.

On October 1, 1993, Polly Klaas, an exuberant twelve-year-old, was kidnapped from her Petaluma, California, home during a slumber party. Her mother, Eve Nichols, was asleep in a nearby bedroom.

A paroled felon, Richard Allen Davis, who had spent fourteen of his thirty-nine years locked up in prison, was ultimately convicted in the case and sentenced to death. He had entered the house, tied the girls up at knifepoint, and then left with Polly. Police questioned Davis shortly after he took Polly when his car got stuck in a ditch on private property. Unaware that an all points bulletin had been made, or even that the young girl sat nearby too scared to scream, the officials let him go.

No one knows for sure when Davis strangled Polly, but indications are it was soon after the kidnapping. He stashed her body under some debris near an abandoned sawmill thirty miles north of Petaluma. A palm print Davis left in Polly's bedroom helped lead police to him, prompting a confession. He eventually took officials to Polly's decomposed body.

The following year, Polly's father, Marc Klaas, channeled his pain to found the KlaasKids Foundation. The foundation's goals include support for individuals and public education for crime prevention against children; assistance in the recovery of missing children; and support for legislative and regulatory protection for children.

On its website, www.klaaskids.org, the organization outlines its genesis and purpose:

The KlaasKids Foundation was established in 1994 to give meaning to the death of twelve-year-old kidnap and murder victim Polly Hannah Klaas and to create a legacy in her name that would be protective of children for generations to come. Conceived with an initial investment of $2,000 the Foundation's mission is to stop crimes against children.

America's continued evolution is predicated on the unspoken promise of past generations that we will give our children a better world than was given to us. As a country created around the concept of the individual, the worth of the individual and the rights of the individual, our ability to fulfill the promise to our children has allowed America to develop into the most influential and powerful nation in world history. We have more data, knowledge and information than has been compiled in all previous generations combined and how we use it will help determine our fate as a people.

The KlaasKids Foundation believes that we can go far toward fulfilling our mission by distilling the best knowledge and information through a societal approach that extends from the President's Cabinet Table to the family's kitchen table. We can win the war for our children's future by acknowledging that crimes against children deserve a high priority on our national and personal agendas. Then, by forming and promoting partnerships with concerned citizens, the private sector, organizations, law enforcement and legislators we take responsibility to become part of the solution to fighting crime and we can take pride in proactive accomplishments.

While Davis sits on death row in San Quentin Prison, just five miles from Klaas's Sausalito home, the dedicated father works out of Polly's old bedroom on the nonprofit foundation. Klaas advises parents on topics including which authorities to contact, how to deal with news reporters if an abduction occurs, and even how best to collect your kids' DNA samples. He believes fingerprints, photographs, and safety tips are a start, but parents need, most of all, to talk to their kids about protecting themselves.

Klaas became a spokesperson and consultant to the van Dams when their daughter, Danielle, was abducted. Family friends invited Klaas to share his experience with the parents. While there, he freely admitted to originally being driven by rage over the murder of his daughter.

"I could bash his [Davis's] brains out with a baseball bat and eat pizza over his quivering corpse," Klaas said to *The San Diego Union-Tribune.* Shedding added light on the statement, before being sentenced to death, Davis had heartlessly elected to taunt Marc Klaas in the courtroom by saying that just before he killed little Polly, the girl begged him "not to do me like my dad."

But today Klaas is using that anger to stop more children from being abducted and murdered, and to keep the people who are responsible for such crimes behind bars.

"I am the destroyer — I'm driven by anger because of what happened to my kid," Klaas explained. "I don't want the perverts to win; they messed with the wrong person."

It was late afternoon on Friday, July 29, 1994, when seven-year-old Megan Kanka was last seen alive riding her bike near her home in Hamilton, a quiet suburb of Trenton, New Jersey. The following day, Megan's lifeless body was found dumped in a nearby park. Jesse Timmendequas, who lived directly across the street from the Kankas, eventually confessed to the brutal crime, including a vicious sexual assault prior to the murder. He had lured the little girl into his home by asking her if she wanted to see a puppy.

The following Sunday morning, only two days after the killing, the Kankas were returning from the medical examiner's office after identifying their child's body. Outside their home a group of parents had gathered both in support and outrage. Much as the recent abductions have crystallized frustrations today, Megan's murder did so then. Many of the people that day held signs to express their deep feelings:

"Where were Megan's rights?" one read.

"Death penalty," said another.

"The right to know," a third sign stated, a direct response to the fact that only after the murder occurred did the parents and their neighbors learn that Timmendequas was a twice-convicted sex offender living in their midst. Not only that, two of his housemates were convicted sex offenders, also.

The Kankas, who described themselves as intensely private people until that point, stopped and signed a petition. What began was a massive public campaign to help protect other innocent children targeted by repeat sex offenders. Maureen Kanka, who had never given a speech before her daughter's death, would now dedicate her life to changing how lawmakers and parents viewed sex offenders.

The signatures that the Kankas added to that petition on July 31, 1994, would be followed by over 430,000 more before then New Jersey Governor Christine Todd Whitman signed into law strict new guidelines on informing the public about felons. Megan's Law, as it was named, required convicted sex offenders released into the community to register with their local police agency, who in turn could notify the public about the offender's presence. Eighty-nine days after their daughter's death, the Kankas had made a tangible difference, potentially saving other children and parents from the hell they had experienced.

Today, even the U.S. federal government has adopted Megan's Law, and mandates have been passed requiring states to adhere to them or risk losing federal funding. At stake are federal grants that pay for crime prevention and victims' assistance programs in local communities. As a result, all fifty states now have versions of Megan's Law. More than 7,500 sex offenders are registered in New Jersey, the pioneering state, and upward of 375,000 are registered around the country.

The house where little Megan Kanka had been killed was eventually purchased by the community and razed. In its place was built a park, Megan's Place, complete with flowers, wooden benches, and a goldfish pond fed by a small waterfall. In the summer, yellow tiger lilies bloom where Jesse Timmendequas, who now sits on death row, once snuffed out an innocent life.

In July 2001, on that site, New Jersey acting Governor Donald T. DiFrancesco signed a high-tech addition to the law that bears Megan's name: a requirement that the names, addresses, and photographs of certain sex offenders be placed on the Internet. Anyone with a computer and Internet access would be able to download details about sex offenders, including the make, model, and license plate number of cars they drive. The Internet directory answered a call by New Jersey residents who voted overwhelmingly to publish such information on the Internet, updating Megan's Law into the age of technology.

"This Internet site will help and will aid parents . . . to know if there is a dangerous predator living around their children," Maureen Kanka said. "If I had had that knowledge, my daughter would be alive and well today."

On the evening of January 13, 1996, a man working in his backyard heard screams coming from a nearby parking lot of an abandoned Winn-Dixie store. He witnessed a nine-year-old girl being dragged screaming off her pink bicycle and forced into a full-size black pickup truck. Four days later, a dog walker found the Berry Elementary School third-grader's body in a creek. Amber Hagerman's throat had been slashed, and she was naked except for one white sock on her right foot.

Only ten days after their daughter was abducted, Amber's parents, Donna Norris and Richard Hagerman, announced a crusade to toughen sex offender laws. Their efforts eventually formed a group People Against Sex Offenders. By March, U.S. Representative Martin Frost introduced the Amber Hagerman Child Protection Act, which increased the prison sentence of those who commit sex offenses against children. Amber's parents would later testify before members of Congress, urging lawmakers to ensure that perpetrators like the one who took their daughter received the strictest possible sentencing.

The case of Amber Hagerman's abduction also spawned the Amber Alert in October 1996. Because a witness was able to get a description of the car in Amber's case, the idea arose to broadcast future vehicle descriptions through an emergency alert on radio stations, much as the Emergency Alert System gives severe weather information. Drivers, many of whom are listening while on crowded freeways and city roads, are urged to be on the lookout. Eventually, many television stations would join in the broadcasting of the Amber Alert.

Years later, Amber's killer has not been found. At one time, the case was being worked by a task force of forty-fiveinvestigators, thirty FBI agents, and additional personnel on loan from other local agencies. They checked about six thousand tips and cleared a dozen false confessions. That task force disbanded in June 1997, and a rental truck hauled away about a hundred boxes of casebooks to be stored at another city facility. One investigator, Jim Ford, is left to follow up on any further leads, which are few and far between. Occasionally, Ford and Amber's mother, Donna, run into each other at the little girl's gravesite.

But the Amber Alert is alive and well. On Tuesday, October 24, 2001, a new campaign hoping to nationalize the Amber Alert was adopted. The program, which sprang from the local alerts police in Arlington, Texas, had begun using, adopted AMBER as an acronym — America's Missing: Broadcast Emergency Response.

In a media event at the National Press Club, Amber's mother, Donna Norris, joined Tyler Cox, the president of the Dallas/Fort Worth Association of Radio Managers, along with national child advocates, including *America's Most Wanted* host John Walsh, in announcing the new push for wider acceptance of the Amber Alert.

"The Amber Plan is a partnership that could make a big difference in saving children's lives," said Walsh. "I truly believe that if this plan was in place when my six-year-old son, Adam, was kidnapped twenty years ago, it may have saved his life. Time is of the essence. We know the Amber Plan works."

That was proven twice in August 2002.

On Thursday, August 1, a gun-toting man in Southern California abducted Jacqueline Marris and Tamara Brooks, two teenagers, sparking the first use in California of the Amber Alert system. Freeway signs flashed for hours with a description of a white 1980 Ford Bronco driven by kidnapper Roy Ratliffe, a thirty-seven-year-old ex-con on the run from an unrelated rape charge.

Someone who had seen the alert stopped a Kern County deputy and reported spotting a matching Bronco on Highway 178 near Bakersfield. A neighbor of Ratliffe's reported he had seen the suspect driving a vehicle matching the description. Then a highway flagman told police he had just heard the Amber Alert on the radio when a white Bronco flashed by him. The net around Ratliffe was drawing tighter, and police closed in.

On a barren piece of Native American reserve land, police finally trapped Ratliffe, who was possibly minutes away from killing his victims. As deputies screamed for him to get out of the vehicle, he reached for a weapon and then fled on foot. Ratliffe was peppered with bullets and died at the scene. In the backseat of the Bronco were the two teenage girls. They were bound with duct tape and had been raped, but they were alive.

Then, on Tuesday, August 13, one-month-old Nancy Crystal Chavez was abducted from her family's minivan in an Abilene, Texas, Wal-Mart parking lot at 4:30 p.m. Officials scrambled to post notices of the kidnapping on nearly one hundred highway message signs and also on the radio, updating the community with a description of the car the suspect fled in — a '90s turquoise sedan.

The signs, as well as media coverage, generated phone tips to police agencies throughout North Texas. In Quanah, a West Texas town about a hundred miles north of Abilene, a sheriff's deputy stopped a car that matched the description provided by the first statewide Amber Alert.

Little Nancy Chaves was recovered safe and sound.

On October 2, 2002, speaking at a White House conference on missing, exploited, and runaway children, President Bush pledged ten million dollars to develop a national standard for the Amber Alert. Bush also announced a new Amber Alert coordinator at the Justice Department who will work on increasing cooperation among state and local plans and distribute the federal money for training and equipment upgrades. The alert created in Amber Hagerman's memory has now become recognized as one of the most effective tools for finding abducting children.

On April 3, 1997, twelve-year-old Laura Smithers went jogging on the back roads near her family's house in Friendswood, Texas, never to return. Seventeen days later her parents, Gay and Bob, finally learned what had happened. Their daughter's decomposed body was found floating in a pond twelve miles away. Laura had been strangled and possibly sexually assaulted. No one has yet to be charged with the crime.

In the days between Laura's disappearance and the subsequent discovery of her body, the community of Friendswood came together in the face of tragedy to search. More than six thousand volunteers put their own lives on hold to give their time and commitment to join the Laura Recovery Center. The volunteers covered more than eight hundred square miles and launched a nationwide hunt to find the missing child. Many continued to put in long hours even after they suspected that Laura would not be found alive.

When Gay and Bob learned their worst fears had been realized, they somehow managed to find inspiration in the way the men and women of Friendswood had united. The parents founded the Laura Recovery Center Foundation, applying the lessons learned in their search for Laura to other cases of missing children and, occasionally, missing adults.

"Unfortunately, there's a huge need," said Gay Smithers. "We get phone calls on a daily basis of children who are missing."

In 2002, a center-trained team of two thousand volunteers found Danielle van Dam's body along a desert road on February 27. The Laura Recovery Center Foundation was also approached by sheriffs in Mesa County, Colorado, to assist in a search for a mother and daughter who vanished from their home just outside Grand Junction, Colorado. It was the first time that law enforcement officials, rather than relatives, had asked the center for assistance. Then in June 2002, when Elizabeth Smart was abducted at gunpoint from her bedroom, once again the Laura Recovery Center was called in to help.

"We started the foundation to try to address the need to rapidly respond to a missing child," explained Bob Smithers to CNN while involved in the search for Elizabeth. "And one of the tools is the Laura Recovery Center Manual, which was written by the volunteers that searched for Laura. It's just a cookbook set of procedures, lessons learned — manual, if you will — and the whole objective is to get a community up and organized and get searchers out on the ground just as quickly as possible."

The "Laura Recovery Center Manual," an eighty-four page instructional booklet, has become the bible for searchers in missing persons cases nationwide. It highlights the need to coordinate law enforcement, community, and family, and it deals with everything from emotional and spiritual concerns to the logistics of organizing large-scale search parties.

"The LRC Manual describes how to conduct a massive, citizen-directed effort to recover a missing child," reads the introduction. "It is hoped that the experiences and guidelines we share will prove useful in recovering your missing child."

A detailed organizational chart outlines some eight various positions to be filled, all with different but crucial roles. They include search operations, administrative, legal, public affairs, family liaison, and resource management, all under the guidance of a director. The goal is to produce an efficient search machine designed to make the most of every precious minute when a child is abducted. The directions are broken down into sections that include the first six hours, the first seventy-two hours, all the way through to search termination.

Unfortunately, despite the solace that Bob and Gay have found in helping other families in need, most searches end in disappointment. The Laura Recovery Center has provided assistance to families in more than four hundred missing persons cases. Out of those, even with their coordinated attempts, only three kidnapped children have ever been brought home alive.

On the homepage of the Laura Recovery Center's website, there is a link that brings the reader to an anonymous eulogy to Laura. It is a clear and poignant explanation of why, despite the grim statistics, the search for all our stolen children will never end.

In Memory — Laura Kate Smither

I did not know Laura, but I, as did the thousands who joined together in a massive search, felt our love for her grow with every step we took. She became the innocence of our youth, she became our daughter, she became the symbol of everything that was pure and decent in our lives . . . Then we came face to face with the evil that took her life away from us.

But we stood together, housewives and soldiers, retired executives and farm workers, police officers and mechanics; we stood together as citizens of our neighborhood, our town, our state, our nation, our world. We held hands and saw not the evil that tried to rip us apart, but the unity that pulled us together. Nothing will ever come close to replacing Laura's life. We as a nation lost one of our greatest achievements — a child full of hope for all the tomorrows . . . But in her loss, as we gathered in prayer, we gained the knowledge that we can stand together against the evil, that we can support one another, that we can offer one another our love. We found that our strength will not be torn apart by the criminals that kill our children, but instead will be made stronger . . .

And in that common bond we will always share a memory of a sweet, amazing twelve year-old child.

We will never forget you, Laura.

How to Keep Your Child Safe

Of all the various organizations that deal with child abduction and safety issues, the National Center for Missing and Exploited Children has emerged as the single best resource for law enforcement and parents alike. With hundreds of employees working both full-time out of their headquarters in Alexandria, Virginia, and volunteering around the country, the NCMEC is the definitive voice when it comes to tips on how to protect your children.

"We are the premier missing children organization in the country, mandated by Congress to be in existence, with the one and only twenty-four-hour hotline," explains Nancy McBride, the Director of Prevention Education at the NCMEC. "The expertise and quality we bring to the table is unmatched."

McBride has been at the center for more than twenty years, and she explains that nearly everyone there has extensive law enforcement or social service backgrounds. On site are also representatives of the FBI, the secret service, customs, and even the postal service and the ATF.

"This is my heart's work, my life's work," says McBride, echoing the sentiment of everyone at the NCMEC. "Everyone here cares."

First and foremost, McBride believes all parents need to take responsibility for educating and informing their own children. The NCMEC can provide literature and instruction, but then it falls to the parent to make sure that these lessons are taken seriously. For those who worry about scaring their children, McBride points out that we need to confront fear in order to overcome it. Sooner or later, many children will be placed in a dangerous situation. By opening up the channels of communication, lives can be saved.

Of the most important factors to consider, McBride points out that according to a recent study conducted by the Washington State Attorney General's Office, 57 percent of all abductions occur from "opportunity." What that means is that predators rely on finding an available victim, either by hanging out at the video arcade, around the playground, or in public restrooms. These monsters want children, and they go to certain places to find them. Parents have to be vigilant to eliminate a predator's opportunities.

"Kids should not be alone," McBride says bluntly. "People say to me, 'I didn't have to be watched all the time when I was growing up.' Well, guess what, the world's changed."

In the most recently updated literature, McBride writes that the following tips "will help parents lessen the opportunity for abduction and kidnapping and better safeguard their children." Although McBride admits she could write a book on the subject, she urges us "to keep it simple," and the NCMEC provides specific lists with only a few bullet points for parents:

1. Teach your children to run away from danger, never toward it. Danger is anyone or anything that invades their personal space. Teach them to yell loudly — their safety is more important than being polite. Statistics show that predators are looking for an easy victim, and a child who fights will improve his or her chances of survival in the case of an attempted abduction.

2. Never let your children go places alone, and always supervise your young children or make sure there is a trusted adult present to supervise them if you cannot. Make sure your older children always take a friend when they go somewhere. Ideally, children of any age will not be unsupervised. It is extremely rare that a predator attempts to take a child who is being watched by an adult.

3. Know where your children are and who they're with at all times. This includes maintaining accurate phone and address lists. Also, check in with those parents, making sure that adequate supervision exists when a child is out of your care. By being proactive, one parent can encourage others to do the same.

4. Talk openly to your children about safety and encourage them to tell you or a trusted adult if anyone or anything makes them feel frightened, confused, or uncomfortable. This is possibly the key point — teach your children to trust their instincts. If they believe they are at risk, they should know that it is never wrong to express their feelings. Pay attention to your children and listen to them.

5. Practice what you teach by creating "what if" scenarios with your children to make sure they understand the safety message and can use it in a real situation. This includes role-playing scenarios. The more scenarios practiced, the better — remember that predators can be creative. A child who has practiced yelling and running away will be more capable of escaping a bad situation.

6. Consider installing an alarm system in your home with a monitoring feature. Make sure your home is secured with deadbolt locks. Check other access points, such as gates, and make sure they have been secured. Make sure that your home is fully secured before you go to sleep. Have a plan if an intruder tries or does get into your home.

7. Make your children part of securing your home. If you have installed an alarm system, demonstrate it to your children and show them how to make certain that doors and windows are locked. This will not only help calm their fears but also help make them part of your "safety plan" at home. By including them in this process, parents are showing through their actions that safety is of the utmost concern.

8. Have a list of family members who can be contacted in

case of an emergency. Designate a family member or close associate who would be able to fill the role of advisor in case of an emergency. Children should have other adults whom they know they can go to: police officers, other caregivers, or known adults in the neighborhood or at the playground.

9. Know your employees and coworkers. Do background screenings and reference checks on everyone who works at your home, particularly those individuals who care for your children. Often these people will learn an immense amount about your family, and you should also know something about them. McBride explains that this can be accomplished by a simple trip to your local police department. Although laws vary from state to state, if they can't help you, they can direct you to the right place for a background check.

10. Report any suspicious persons or activities to law enforcement — do *not* wait. This is another key point. If a child feels he or she has been targeted or witnesses another child being targeted, time is of the essence. Once again, tell children to trust their instincts. It's always better to err on the side of caution.

"People say they don't want to bother the police if they're wrong," explains McBride. "But what if they're right? Chances are that if your child escaped, that predator will go and find another victim."

In addition to these rules for parents, the NCMEC provides a list specifically for children. These should be written out and placed where they can be seen on a regular basis, such as the refrigerator. Predators don't take vacations, McBride points out, so neither can we when it comes to safety. These are written in the first person specifically to emphasize to children their own crucial responsibilities when it comes to safety.

1. I always check first with my parents or the person in charge before I go anywhere or get into a car, even with someone I know.

2. I always check first with my parents or a trusted adult before I accept anything from anyone, even from someone I know.

3. I always take a friend with me when I go places or play outside.

4. I know my name, address, telephone number, and my parents' names.

5. I say no if someone tries to touch me or treat me in a way that makes me feel scared, uncomfortable, or confused.

6. I know that I can tell my parents or a trusted adult if I feel scared, uncomfortable, or confused.

7. It's okay to say no, and I know that there will always be someone who can help me.

8. I am strong, smart, and have the right to be safe.

The wording of two of these rules addresses one of the hardest topics for both children and parents. Most predators are after a child to satisfy one thing — a twisted sexual desire. Children should know that *anything* that makes them "scared, uncomfortable, or confused" must be discussed. But by following these rules, by helping a child to feel more comfortable about discussing and confronting these safety issues, all can ultimately feel more secure.

"Wouldn't it be nice if we could pick out the predator?" McBride asks. "Wouldn't it be great if they wore a sign? Well, they don't. People owe it to their children, to themselves, to be safer, especially these days. How many times have we heard of kids falling for the 'puppy lore'? Teach them there is no puppy. Don't fall for it!"

"If there's a good thing that has come of all these high-profile cases, it's that parents are becoming more aware and they're taking the time to sit down with kids to let them know in a nonthreatening way about safety," adds Ben Armini, a case manager for the Missing Children's Division of the NCMEC. Armini has twenty-five years of law enforcement experience and is also a graduate of the FBI Academy at Quantico. "Just like we tell kids to look both ways before they cross the street, we need to tell them about these things."

After emphasizing prevention, Armini describes the Amber Alert as one of the most effective tools available today for law enforcement to locate a child if an abduction has already occurred. The NCMEC, which originally promoted nationalization of the plan in late 2001, has now successfully pushed President Bush to allocate federal funds for that purpose.

"The Amber Alert is so logical," says Armini. "Exactly as a serious weather alert is given, we tell the public about a missing child. As we've seen, those first few hours are crucial, and this plan works. It has already saved over thirty children."

Armini explains that parents can call their local law enforcement agencies and urge them to adopt Amber Alert plans. The NCMEC will provide an Amber Alert handbook and a training tape. And if a child is already missing and a parent is unsure if their local law enforcement is equipped to enact an Amber Alert, they can always call the NCMEC for help.

Ann Scofield heads up the NCMEC's Project Alert division, which is comprised of hundreds of retired law enforcement personnel from around the country who volunteer to assist local police departments when a child is missing. Scofield spent twenty-five years with the L.A. County Sheriff's Department before joining the center. From making and distributing posters to adding their experienced insight into a specific investigation, the members of Project Alert are trained to do whatever it takes to assist in a recovery effort.

Scofield points out that the Project Alert representatives are also available to visit schools or other civic organizations to teach prevention education. They will come, free of charge, with NCMEC literature and pamphlets to locations around the country. They can provide specific presentations geared either to parents or to children.

"The one central message is: Don't ignore educating the child," says Scofield. "Inevitably, a child will be placed in a situation where they have to make decisions themselves. They have to be prepared when that time comes."

Some parents may feel that these precautions begin to go too far, but Scofield counters, "The risk is your leaving your child vulnerable to a predator." Today, the risks of not taking precautions are just too great.

If parents need any more evidence of this, consider a few of the crimes that the NCMEC has helped to prevent. Dealing specifically with the sexual exploitation of children, the center operates a "CyberTipline" in partnership with the Federal Bureau of Investigation, the U.S. Customs Service, the U.S. Postal Inspection Service, and state and local law enforcement agencies. The U.S. Congress has also funded these initiatives, and they have already put a dent in the proliferation of child pornography and prevented planned assaults.

On June 11, 2000, the CyberTipline received an urgent tip from a woman in Dubuque, Iowa, who detailed an intended abduction that was to take place on June 14th involving a fifty-three-year-old Indiana man who had been corresponding via the Internet with a fourteen-year-old girl from Wisconsin. The caller went on to say that the girl intended to run away with the suspect, who expected to have sexual relations with the child.

Recognizing the immediate danger, CyberTipline analysts alerted the Internet Crimes Against Children Task Force in Wisconsin, as well as law enforcement agencies in both Iowa and Indiana. When the suspect arrived at the designated meeting place, a shopping mall in Madison, Wisconsin, he was arrested and charged with attempted child enticement; attempted child abduction; attempted interference with parental custody; possession of marijuana; possession of drug paraphernalia; and, after putting up a fight at the scene, criminal damage to property.

Authorities then searched the man's truck and found a twelve-inch ax, pieces of rope, Demerol pills, and illegal drug paraphernalia. The suspect's criminal record included a 1968 conviction for second-degree murder. He was convicted of all six charges against him and sentenced to twenty-four years in prison with a minimum of fourteen to be served.

On November 8, 2000, the CyberTipline received another tip from a New Zealand law enforcement agency. The information concerned an anonymous Internet user expressing an interest both in sexual activity with minors and child pornography. Via e-mail correspondence with a New Zealand detective posing under an assumed identity, the suspect outlined his desire to have sex with a preteen female, specifically on North America's West Coast.

Staffers from NCMEC's Exploited Child Unit alerted the Los Angeles Police Department. An LAPD detective, posing as an adult with access to children for sexual purposes, established e-mail contact with the suspect, who explicitly outlined the types of activities he wished to perform with young children. New Zealand agents then determined that the suspect, a twenty-seven-year-old Canadian resident, was willing to travel to California for sex with a child.

On May 19, 2001, the suspect met the undercover detective in a Los Angeles motel room, where he paid $150 for access to a fictitious twelve-year-old girl. He was arrested and later charged with six felony counts, including attempted lewd acts with a child, possessing obscene materials, and employing a child for obscene purposes. Searches of the motel room revealed further evidence, such as sexual paraphernalia, pornographic videotapes, and explicit written descriptions of what he intended to do to the little girl.

Upon searching the man's house, Canadian law enforcement discovered electronic evidence on his computer as well as photographs of potential victims — all children. Various Canadian agencies are now trying to identify the subjects in the pictures and are also investigating a potential link between this suspect and the perpetrator of an attempted kidnapping in his community where his appearance closely matches the composite sketch of the abductor. He is currently awaiting a preliminary hearing in California.

"Never allow a child to have a computer in a secret place," concluded Scofield. There have been too many such examples of predators using the Internet to entice potential victims. "Set up computers in the family room, where parents can oversee what children are doing on the Net." Scofield adds that many companies offer software that can prevent unsuspecting children from venturing into certain chat rooms and websites.

Donald and Mary Sprague are a husband-and-wife Project Alert team who work under the direction of Scofield at the NCMEC. They are both retired from the Saganaw, Michigan, police force.

"These crimes touch the very innocence of our society," explains Mary about her commitment to the center. "Children are the members of our society we need to protect the most. We want to get the word out to law enforcement and parents that we're here to help. The center is a phenomenal place, where the children are number one. We are here, free of charge, to educate and, God forbid something happens, help a family to cope."

For more information, call the National Center for Missing and Exploited Children at 1-800-THE LOST (1-800-843-5678), or visit its website at www.missingkids.com. The CyberTipline can be reached by calling the same number, or by visiting its website at www.cybertipline.com. There is no concern too small or too great for the NCMEC when it comes to protecting our children.

"The NCMEC will be here, twenty-four hours a day, 365 days a year," concludes Nancy McBride. "These tragedies can be overwhelming, but the good guys can and will make this world a better place for children."